Continuing Challenges and Potential for Collaborative Approaches to Education Reform

Susan J. Bodilly, Rita Karam, Nate Orr

Sponsored by the Ford Foundation

EDUCATION

The research in this report was produced within RAND Education, a unit of the RAND Corporation. The research was sponsored by the Ford Foundation.

Library of Congress Cataloging-in-Publication Data is available for this publication.

ISBN 978-0-8330-5152-3

Published 2011 by the RAND Corporation
1776 Main Street, P.O. Box 2138, Santa Monica, CA 90407-2138
1200 South Hayes Street, Arlington, VA 22202-5050
4570 Fifth Avenue, Suite 600, Pittsburgh, PA 15213-2665
RAND URL: http://www.rand.org/
To order RAND documents or to obtain additional information, contact
Distribution Services: Telephone: (310) 451-7002;
Fax: (310) 451-6915; Email: order@rand.org

Preface

In 1997, the Ford Foundation began an effort, called the Collaborating for Education Reform Initiative (CERI), to promote school improvement in communities. It funded eight sites to establish collaboratives of community-based organizations and local school districts that were to create and sustain education reforms in their local areas. As part of this effort, the foundation sponsored a formative assessment of the grantees' progress, to be carried out by the RAND Corporation from 1999 to 2003. The assessment was documented in *Challenges and Potential of a Collaborative Approach to Education Reform* (Bodilly, Chun, et al., 2004).

In 2004, the foundation dropped five sites and added two new sites to the initiative. RAND continued to track the progress made toward the grantees' goals from 2004 to 2009. This monograph documents the progress made by the grantees during that time period.

The audiences for this monograph are policymakers involved in trying to build sustained support for educational improvement and practitioners interested in using collaborative efforts among community organizations to improve public educational services.

This research was conducted by RAND Education, a unit of the RAND Corporation.

Contents

Tables

Summary

Introduction

After years of grant making, Ford Foundation staff strongly believed that a school district central office could not reform itself; rather, they believed that reform could be promoted by relying on collaborations among organizations *outside* the district central office to sustain reform. This belief grew out of other foundations' experiences with collaborative efforts and the Ford Foundation's own previous efforts at collaborative formation from 1991 to 2000 in the Urban Partnership Program (UPP). Thus, the foundation wanted to promote an education reform strategy based on *local collaboration among community organizations*.

Based on these premises, the foundation began a new initiative in 1997–1998—the Collaborating for Education Reform Initiative (CERI)—by issuing grants to organizations in eight communities and providing the sites with funds, guidance, and technical assistance to develop collaboratives and carry out activities to improve teaching and learning. CERI's collaborative activities were directed at three possible community groups: the district, a feeder pattern or cluster of schools in a district, and the larger community, such as parents and voters.

In 1999, the foundation asked the RAND Corporation to formatively assess CERI to provide sites with feedback to improve their efforts, provide information to inform the foundation's decisions about support and funding to grantees, and document the challenges and possible successes of this approach to school improvement. During this period, RAND tracked the sites' progress toward CERI's goals and reported on the first five years of the effort in 2004 (Bodilly, Chun, et al., 2004).

In 2004, the foundation reorganized CERI by dropping five of the original eight grantees and adding two new ones (for a total of five):

- the Alianza Metropolitana de San Juan Para La Educación in San Juan, Puerto Rico. This collaborative of several community-based organizations (CBOs) and a major university sought to promote student achievement by *scaling up a school improvement model developed under CERI 1 and demonstrated in Catano, Puerto Rico, and by creating the first education policy institute on the island.*
- Ask for More (AFM) in Jackson, Mississippi. This new collaborative was created in response to CERI 1 and led by a CBO called Parents for Public Schools (PPS) that chose to promote student achievement by *developing and demonstrating best practices in a specific feeder pattern and then scaling these up to the district.*
- Austin Interfaith (AI) in Austin, Texas. This CBO with ties to church congregations is dedicated to improving the lives of underserved minorities and proposed work with other CBOs to *build a teacher pipeline to provide high-quality teachers to hard-to-staff schools.*
- DC VOICE in Washington, D.C. This private, nonprofit organization was created during CERI 1 with the goal of *providing research-based advocacy for improving the supports offered in the district for improved teacher quality.*
- Grow Your Own (GYO) in Chicago, Illinois. This combination of CBOs led by the Association of Community Organizations for Reform Now (ACORN) proposed to *develop a pipeline of high-quality teachers for hard-to-staff schools.*

This new incarnation of CERI went forward with these five grantees until 2009. With the restructuring, the foundation emphasized collaborative activities designed to affect district and state education policies but, unlike in CERI 1, offered very little technical assistance to the sites. The foundation expected the collaborative activities to result in changes in teaching and learning in the schools in the local school districts. Specifically, the foundation had laid down a new set of goals for the five sites:

- Develop interorganizational linkages to the point of becoming a well-functioning collaborative and achieve financial independence.
- Develop and implement plans for improving the quality of teaching and learning.
- Develop and implement plans for systemic changes in policy to support improved teaching and learning.
- Develop a unique voice for underserved communities outside of the central office to air concerns about educational services.

Our Research Purpose and Approach

In 2004, the foundation asked RAND to track the sites' progress toward CERI's new goals and provide feedback to the foundation and the five grantees, documenting any lessons that others might learn from this effort. The research questions addressed from 2004 to 2009 were as follows:

1. Did grantees show progress toward desired outcomes?
   a. Did they develop collaborative interorganizational linkages and find sustainable funding?
   b. Did they choose reasonable interventions that might be expected to have impact?
   c. Did they make progress in promoting teaching and learning, in promoting policy initiatives, and in acting as a "voice in the community"?
2. What lessons or promising practices resulted from the experiences of individual collaboratives or the group as a whole?
3. Did the foundation create financially sustainable collaboratives that can promote education improvement?

To help answer these research questions, we chose a replicated case-study approach, viewing each collaborative and its surrounding community as a single embedded case. We collected and analyzed data from multiple sources—including extensive field interviews; documents, such as newspaper articles and printed materials provided by collaborative members; and limited administrative data supplied by districts and schools. These data were organized thematically in relation to the research questions and synthesized to identify common and contrasting themes across the sites.

Findings

Here, we present the key findings in relation to the three research questions.

Research Question 1: Did Grantees Show Progress Toward Desired Outcomes?

Overall, we found that the second CERI effort (CERI 2) resulted in several functioning collaboratives but that those collaboratives' ability to meet their goals varied widely, something that emerges when we look more specifically at the three suboutcomes.

Did They Develop Collaborative Interorganizational Linkages and Find Sustainable Funding? At the end of the study in 2009, AI appeared to be largely self-sustaining and growing in terms of linking up to new groups to positively influence policy at the state and local levels in Texas and in terms of taking on new initiatives. Because of a very difficult state environment for nonprofits and an inability to gain traction in a very rapidly changing environment, the Alianza was functioning as a "network of CBOs" interested in reform rather than as a collaborative. The other three sites appeared to be in a state of "reflection and planning," having accomplished some goals but being in the process of deciding "where to go from here." Chicago's GYO and Washington's DC VOICE had some ability to sustain themselves, and each was actively pursuing an agenda with partners. The Jackson AFM collaborative could not be sustained without external funding and had not identified such sources successfully.

Did They Choose Reasonable Interventions That Might Be Expected to Have Impact? The sites had difficulty choosing appropriate interventions that showed promise in having an impact on student performance and in being able to be scaled up. Although all five sites appropriately identified the needs of the schools in their communities, the interventions they selected to address the problems were often not clearly connected to a research literature showing proven results. Furthermore, many of the interventions, such as the development and implementation of a teacher pipeline targeting school and community members in poor inner-city areas, required resources and time beyond the period of the foundation grant to fully implement and show empirical results, which posed significant challenges, especially when they were asked to become self-sustaining in the recessionary market of 2008–2009.

Did They Make Progress in Promoting Teaching and Learning, in Promoting Policy Initiatives, and in Acting as a "Voice in the Community"? In terms of making progress toward promoting teaching and learning, only three of the sites—AI, the Alianza, and AFM—chose interventions that were somewhat designed to have a direct impact on teaching and learning. Usually, these interventions included professional development for leaders, teachers, counselors, and parents. One exception was AI's effort to create a cluster of district schools, with greater flexibility and autonomy than other schools in the district. The sites also varied in their ability to implement their chosen interventions, and those interventions' impact on teaching and learning also varied by site. By 2007, the Alianza stopped providing professional development to its districts, and respondents there noted that the Alianza's long-term impact was insignificant. AI's efforts to create an independent cluster of schools failed to be approved, but AFM was able to promote principal collaboration and articulate greater vertical alignment of district curriculum.

All the sites attempted to affect state or local policies to support quality teaching and learning. Two of the grantees—AI and AFM—showed significant progress in this area, especially in terms of changing school behaviors. Working with others (e.g., sister organizations, teacher unions, churches), AI influenced the state legislature to pass a bill that limited the percentage of time that schools were allowed to spend on testing students, thus directly affecting teacher behavior. Interventions implemented by AFM in a high school feeder pattern known as the Lanier cluster were adopted by the school district. Another intervention in AFM involved principal-to-principal collaboration within a feed pattern, which produced changes in how school leaders collaborated and shared information.

GYO ran a grassroots organizing campaign, successfully ensuring the passage of an Illinois initiative to develop and implement a teacher pipeline. However, this policy's effectiveness at improving student outcomes depended on many factors, including the retention rate of teacher candidates and the length of time to their graduation and placement in Chicago schools. At the time of our last visit, in 2009, the teacher pipeline's impact on teaching and learning was not promising. None of the GYO candidates had graduated and started teaching in Chicago public schools. In fact, many were still taking classes at the community college level.

DC VOICE's efforts to affect policy diminished over time because of the mayoral takeover of the District of Columbia Public Schools (DCPS) in 2007. Finally, the Alianza had not established a viable, well-functioning policy institute, which was a major goal of its grant.

When we look at the collaboratives becoming a voice for the underserved and underrepresented, only AI became a strong voice in education reform at both the local and state levels through its partnership with other strong organizations and community mobilizing efforts. Two other sites made progress, but on a lesser scale. DC VOICE developed and engaged leaders from underserved populations in educational issues through mobilizing activities within the District of Columbia. AFM became the voice of the community on specific issues pertaining to collaborative approaches.

Research Question 2: What Lessons or Promising Practices Resulted from the Experiences of Individual Collaboratives or the Group as a Whole?

Looking across the sites, we identified several themes pertaining to building and sustaining collaboratives; promoting quality teaching, learning, and policy initiatives; and developing the voice of reform.

The study found that the sites' abilities to develop and sustain strong collaboratives were facilitated by several factors, including strong leadership that could promote shared goals among the members, a positive funding environment, and the ability to produce information, funding, and progress that were valuable to members and stakeholders. Several factors hindered collaborative development and sustainment, the most crucial of which was a severe change in the financial environment.

Furthermore, collaboratives that were able to influence teaching and learning or educational policies were those that had amiable relationships with the central office or strong stakeholder support (or both). Other factors identified as critical for promoting teaching and learning include the adoption of "reasonable" interventions that were proven to be effective and aligned with identified educational goals and contextual needs, selection of interventions aligned with collaborative expertise, continuous monitoring of the performance of interventions, and the use of collaborative approaches for implementing interventions.

Regarding the development of constituency voice, factors the study identified as important include collaboratives' consistency of and adherence to their mission over time to increase public confidence in their work, and collaboratives' involvement of a broad segment of the community that has legitimacy and power in the education policy arena.

Research Question 3: Did the Foundation Create Financially Sustainable Collaboratives That Can Promote Education Improvement?

In answer to the last research question, we conclude that collaboratives can be deliberately formed with support by outside funders, such as the Ford Foundation. However, it is not a straightforward process, and the financial sustainability of the grantees' initiatives remained highly uncertain in the recessionary environment.

Lessons from this effort point to actions that foundations and collaboratives might take to ensure a more-successful effort, especially in uncertain environments. Specifically, we suggest that future efforts at collaborative formation promote the following actions:

- More-clearly communicate expectations at the start of the initiative and more-carefully consider the alignment between goals, interventions, available resources, and the time frame of the initiative.
- Make use of data to diagnose problems, conduct strategic planning, develop activities, and provide feedback, especially during the planning stages.
- Conduct more-routine and regular meetings and promote data sharing across sites aimed at providing opportunities to learn about progress in general and comparative progress.
- Pay attention early on to future fundraising by the collaboratives, and provide foundation supports for these efforts.
- Foster the development of a foundation collaborative process and the adoption of such processes by collaborative leaders.

Adopting these suggestions cannot guarantee strong progress, but doing so might enable stronger collaborative formation.

Acknowledgments

We wish to thank the many people who contributed to this work.

The Ford Foundation program officers were a major source of inspiration and insight during this project. Janice Petrovich and Cyrus Driver from the foundation, in particular, provided guidance and support.

The project could not have been completed without the significant help of the members of each of the collaboratives studied, especially their leaders. In addition, schools involved with the collaboratives opened their doors to us to help study the impact of implemented activities. Districts provided us with significant support in terms of data and time. We thank all of them for their support and contributions.

The monograph continues the work summarized in a previous report (Bodilly, Chun, et al., 2004). Some basic methodological material and synopsis of the initial years of the initiative are taken from that document, and we wish to thank the authors for their contributions to the groundwork of this second study.

Several members of the RAND staff contributed greatly to the work contained within this monograph, including Dahlia Lichter and Alice Taylor. Much of this monograph's value rests on their contributions.

Reviewers played an important role throughout this project. These included Amanda Datnow of the University of California, San Diego; Julie Marsh of the University of Southern California; and Cathy Stasz of RAND. We thank them for their insights and efforts to make our work better. Although they helped improve the monograph, the final contents are the responsibility solely of the authors.

Abbreviations

ACORN	Association of Community Organizations for Reform Now
AFM	Ask for More
AI	Austin Interfaith
AISD	Austin Independent School District
CBO	community-based organization
CCC	Cross City Campaign for Urban School Reform
CERI	Collaborating for Education Reform Initiative
CPS	Chicago Public Schools
DCPS	District of Columbia Public Schools
DECCES	Demonstrative District for the Systemic Change in Education
DFC	Design for Change
FRL	free and reduced-price lunch
FY	fiscal year
GYO	Grow Your Own
IPEDCo	Institute of Educational Policy for Community Development

ISBE   Illinois State Board of Education

JPS   Jackson Public Schools

LCN   Learning Communities Network

LEP   limited English proficiency

LSNA   Logan Square Neighborhood Association

LVCDC   Little Village Community Development Corporation

MOU   memorandum of understanding

PEN   Public Education Network

PLI   Parent Leadership Institute

PPS   Parents for Public Schools

PRCF   Puerto Rico Community Foundation

PTA   parent-teacher association

RFP   request for proposals

SQT   Supports for Quality Teaching

UPP   Urban Partnership Program

CHAPTER ONE

Introduction

The Ford Foundation, frustrated with past attempts at encouraging the improvement of educational services in U.S. inner cities, began an initiative it hoped would bring about more-sustained change. The foundation called its effort the Collaborating for Education Reform Initiative (CERI). From 1997 through 2003, it funded eight collaborative efforts in selected cities in the hope of developing and sustaining educational improvement. In 2004, it restructured CERI to support five collaborative efforts and began what it referred to as *CERI 2.*

The remainder of this chapter provides the reader with the foundation's rationale for the original CERI and the following CERI 2, the role RAND played, and the purpose of the research and the general approach RAND took to examine CERI 2. Finally, it outlines the rest of this monograph.

Background on the Initiative

The Ford Foundation advanced a vision of education reform to improve the educational achievement of a large number of students and promote system-wide changes in policies and practices. The intent of CERI was specifically *to improve the quality of teaching and learning in classrooms and schools in fundamental ways in order to increase student outcomes.*

CERI differed from many other education reform initiatives in two ways. First, the foundation believed that central district offices lacked the ability to improve teaching and learning because central district offices

1

- made poor choices in selecting interventions to address the problems faced
- lacked consistency of vision due to politics, leadership turnover, and lack of stakeholder buy-in
- were overly influenced by large, entrenched bureaucracies that prevented change from occurring
- had unreliable inputs, such as unstable funding and political will, that made reform efforts uncertain.

CERI, therefore, called for the formation of collaboratives composed of community-based organizations (CBOs) to address systemic barriers to high-quality teaching and learning. CERI based education reform outside central district offices.

Second, the initiative called for multipronged interventions to effect change in teaching and learning. Through internal discussions and examination of existing initiatives, the foundation staff became convinced that cities could make high-quality teaching in all classrooms a reality by utilizing a combination of approaches: effectively linking the different levels of pre-K through 12 and higher-education systems; promoting informed public dialogue, debate, and consensus building around school reform options; promoting professional development for faculty, staff, and administrators; promoting district and state policy changes; and enhancing the role of parents and caregivers. In order to affect teaching and learning, the foundation believed that these approaches should be coherent, steady, and coordinated.

The History of CERI 1 (1998–2003)

From 1989 to 1991, the foundation supported an Urban Partnership Program (UPP). The aim of this program was to promote collaboration among colleges and universities to improve minority student access to college. At the end of this initiative, the foundation program officers concluded that the idea of developing collaborative efforts among community organizations had merit, but they now wished to focus on grades K–12 in urban school districts.

Starting in 1997, the foundation began CERI, a grant-making strategy of supporting the formation of collaboratives composed of

CBOs and other groups in urban settings to address systemic barriers to high-quality teaching and learning in grades K–12. It began with planning grants to each selected grantee and then provision of awards of an average of $300,000 per year (the grant amount varied by site) for a period of five years in implementation grants. Three of these (Miami, Puerto Rico, and Santa Ana) were former UPP collaboratives that reorganized to apply for these funds. The funds were to be used to develop collaboratives to unite the CBOs, schools, and their respective districts in ways that could produce greater levels of improvement and a stronger, more-consistent focus on the reform agenda. The foundation understood that the funding level was not enough to underwrite major reforms in any of these communities but thought that it was enough to support collaborative efforts.

In fall 1999, the Ford Foundation asked RAND to track the progress of the grantees toward the broad goals of the effort and capture any lessons that might be useful to other cities. In the early years of the effort, the goals remained unwritten and somewhat vague. By 2001, with the assistance of RAND, the foundation specified four major goals: the development of a functioning collaborative; the development of activities to promote improved teaching and learning; the development of strategies for sustainment; and the ability to show impact on important student outcomes. Progress was to be assessed in line with these goals.

From 1998 to 2003, the foundation provided for technical assistance for the grantees through the services of Learning Communities Network (LCN), a private, nonprofit organization based in Cleveland that offered such services as strategic planning, program development, and data analysis to CBOs. In addition, the foundation convened the grantees, sometimes twice a year, to share insights, encourage each other, and to hear RAND and LCN's feedback. Guest speakers were often provided. A RAND report documents the experiences of CERI grantees during this period (Bodilly, Chun, et al., 2004).

The History of CERI 2 (2004–2009)

In 2003, after five years, the foundation considered the grantees' progress and accomplishments and found some to be seriously lacking.

Using the initial RAND study and foundation findings, the foundation program officers restructured the effort to fund five grantees, three from CERI 1 and two emerging collaboratives, to 2009. The three original grantees were the Alianza Metropolitana de San Juan Para La Educación in Puerto Rico; Ask for More (AFM) in Jackson, Mississippi; and DC VOICE in Washington, D.C., and the new grantees were Grow Your Own (GYO) in Chicago, Illinois, and Austin Interfaith (AI) in Austin, Texas. These two new grantees had been given planning grants in August 2002. As with CERI 1, the grantees were provided about $300,000 per year to develop collaboratives to promote education reform. RAND continued tracking all grantees' progress toward the foundation's goals.

In addition to different grantees, CERI 2 encompassed other changes, partly due to changing circumstances within the foundation. By the beginning of CERI 2, the number of staff in the foundation dedicated to the U.S. education program was reduced from five to two. Still managing a large portfolio, their attention to CERI 2 waned. In the last year of CERI, the senior education manager retired as well, leaving one staff person to manage the entire portfolio. Second, the foundation undertook a new initiative dedicated to arts integration in schools. The attention of the CERI 2 program officer was clearly split between arts integration and CERI 2. Third, the foundation's president retired, and the new president immediately began a strategic review of programming. For the final two years of CERI 2, the foundation was heavily involved in a restructuring effort. For the last year of CERI 2, the foundation, like others, began to experience the effects of the worst recession in U.S. history, and the strategic review took on new importance.

Several other changes occurred that affected what the grantees attempted. First, the grantees were no longer encouraged to have direct, cluster-level activities, in large part because these were seen as unsustainable given the level of foundation funding and were directly subsidizing activities for which districts would otherwise be paying, such as professional development.

Second, grantees were encouraged to focus some efforts on changing policy and developing a "voice in the community." Foundation staff had become interested in the growing "community-organizing" movement, especially as regards education reform. Authors, such as Shirley (1997) and Warren (2001), described community-organizing efforts in different locales across the country and their impact on education. Foundation staff, with backgrounds in community organizing in Chicago, were intrigued with this work and encouraged sites to move in this direction. (We note that the two new grantees from Austin and Chicago were heavily featured in this literature and major developers of community-organizing efforts.)

In addition, the foundation staff recognized from CERI 1 that many of the interventions that grantees chose could only indirectly affect student test scores or would do so only in the long term—well outside the timeline envisioned for the effort. The foundation signaled that it would no longer hold the grantees accountable for improving test scores but still expected grantees to choose interventions that could logically hope to positively affect student performance. It asked grantees and RAND to track school performance over time.

In essence, the foundation had laid down a new set of goals with CERI 2:

- Develop interorganizational linkages to the point of becoming a well-functioning collaborative and achieving financial independence.
- Develop and implement plans for improving the quality of teaching and learning.
- Develop and implement plans for systemic changes in policy to support improved teaching and learning.
- Develop a unique voice for underserved communities outside of the central office to air concerns about educational services.

While still active in the first two years of CERI 2, by 2006, the LCN technical-assistance activities were discontinued. Following 2006, the foundation increased the amount of awards provided to each site by $50,000 to help the sites purchase their own technical assistance if needed.

The grantees' lead agencies, major organizational partners, and major focus are shown in Table 1.1. The grantees were all led by CBOs and were located in cities with considerable variation in size and demographics (see Table 1.2).

Purpose and Approach

In 2004, RAND undertook a five-year progress assessment of the CERI 2 effort that had three purposes: to provide feedback to sites to improve their efforts, to provide information to the foundation to inform its decisions about support and funding provided to sites, and to document the progress made under this collaborative initiative. The research questions were as follows:

1. Did grantees show progress toward desired outcomes?
   a. Did they develop collaborative interorganizational linkages and find sustainable funding?
   b. Did they choose reasonable interventions that might be expected to have impact?
   c. Did they make progress in promoting teaching and learning, in promoting policy initiatives, and in acting as a "voice in the community"?
2. What lessons or promising practices resulted from the experiences of individual collaboratives or the group as a whole?
3. Did the initiative create financially sustainable collaboratives that can promote education improvement?

CERI is a development effort suitable for study using qualitative approaches, including descriptive analysis. In our effort to assess collaborative formation and the progress made toward desired outcomes, we chose a replicated case-study approach, with each set of grantees and its surrounding community being a single embedded case. The unit of analysis was the collaborative effort and its impact on the educational improvement within its community. We collected and analyzed primarily qualitative data on progress. Our analysis compared grantee

Table 1.1
Collaboratives' Original Descriptions, 2003–2005 Plans

Collaborative Name	The Alianza	AFM	AI	DC VOICE	GYO
Location	Puerto Rico	Jackson, Miss.	Austin, Texas	Washington, D.C.	Chicago, Ill.
Lead agency/fiscal agent, if different	Sacred Heart University (San Juan, P.R.)	PPS	AI	DC VOICE	ACORN
Other major partners	Aspira, College Board, P.R. Department of Education, P.R. Community Foundation	Principals of Lanier cluster	Austin Community College, St. Edwards University, Capital Idea	Not applicable	CCC, LSNA
Focus of effort	Promote student achievement through the adoption of the school improvement model developed in CERI 1	Promote student achievement by adopting best practices across the Lanier cluster	Build a teacher pipeline to provide high-quality teachers to hard-to-staff schools	Provide research-based advocacy for improving the supports for teacher quality	Build a teacher pipeline to staff hard-to-staff schools and reduce teacher turnover
CERI 1 site	Yes, and a member of Ford original UPP	Yes	No	Yes	No

NOTE: PPS = Parents for Public Schools. ACORN = Association of Community Organizations for Reform Now. CCC = Cross City Campaign for Urban School Reform. LSNA = Logan Square Neighborhood Association.

Table 1.2
CERI 2 Sites Started with Significant Variation (characteristics in 2002–2003)

Characteristic	The Alianza (Cataño, P.R., 1998)	AFM (Jackson, Miss., 1999)	AI (Austin, Texas, 2003)	DC VOICE (Washington, D.C., 1999)	GYO (Chicago, Ill., 2004)
Area economy	Stagnant	Stagnant	Growth	Growth	Mixed
Cluster economy	Stagnant	Stagnant	No cluster	No cluster	No cluster
Enrollment	5,100	31,579 C = 4,661	78,155	67,522	426,040
FRL (%)	90	85 C = 91	53	65	85
LEP (%)	N/A	None	21	8	15
Majority student language spoken in the home	Spanish	English	Multiple	Multiple	Multiple

NOTE: C = cluster. FRL = free and reduced-price lunch. LEP = limited English proficiency. N/A = not applicable.

progress toward goals specified by the foundation; we also compared grantees' progress with that of other grantees, looking for insights into why some made more progress than others.

Remainder of the Monograph

In Chapter Two, we provide a conceptual framework based in the literature and the indicators of progress and methodology used to assess collaborative development. Chapter Three addresses the progress that each grantee made toward building a functioning collaborative and includes a short synopsis of the progress of the UPP sites that predated the CERI 1 and 2 programs. Chapter Four describes what each grantee attempted to do, whether the literature supports that grantee's approach as a reasonable one to improving teaching and learning, and assesses progress made across the grantees organized around the Ford goals. The final chapter provides conclusions, especially answering the third question posed, and recommendations.

CHAPTER TWO

Approach, Concepts, and Development of Indicators

In this chapter, we discuss important concepts used in the course of this study. We first provide more details on the study approach and methods. We then review the literature for important insights and definitions. Finally, we discuss the key indicators used to judge the grantees' progress toward CERI 2's goals.

Approach

We chose a qualitative case-study analysis approach for two reasons. First, the phenomena we were observing were complex and unfolding, and we had no ability to control the fluid situation. The research questions were primarily concerned with description of progress and how progress was made, lending themselves to qualitative description. Second, the complexity of the undertaking observed created more variables of interest than could be supported by a quantitative analysis of five sites.

To ensure consistency in data collection, we used a replicated case-study approach, with each collaborative and its surrounding community as a single embedded case. The unit of analysis was the collaborative and its efforts at improvement within its community.

Although the foundation's ultimate outcome of interest is student learning, there were four main reasons that it was not feasible for this study to assess the impact of the collaboratives' efforts on student learning. First, the sites' efforts, approved by the foundation in the proposal process, were often indirectly and very distally related to student outcomes in time. For example, in Austin and Chicago, the grantees intended to develop teacher pipelines using school and community members who would enter college to obtain their teaching degree, a process that would minimally take four years and possibly take significantly longer. The newly minted teachers would then enter the community schools and, the grantees hoped, change pedagogy and attitudes in the schools as well as more-adeptly teach youngsters whose backgrounds and challenges they were uniquely fitted to address. In total, it would likely take eight years to do such an evaluation: a year to develop the program and recruit the first cohort, four years minimally to see the first graduates, and at least two years of teaching to measure impact.

Second, the possible impact of some of the interventions would fall on too few people to construct a valid sample to test quantitative impacts. For example, in the teacher pipeline examples, upon entry in the schools, the number of teachers in the cohort, at least according to the plans developed, would be so small as to not provide an adequate sample size on which to base any analysis of test-score gain comparisons.

Third, it is difficult to disentangle the effects of the intervention of interest (those adopted by the collaborative) from the effects of other influencers of student outcomes, such as major state and national reforms undertaken in this same time frame or local programs, such as improved district-based staff development.

Finally and related, the collaboratives' efforts at change often overlapped with those of other organizations, such as other CBOs, making it difficult to disentangle the cause of any student effects. For example, DC VOICE planned to advocate for specific changes to teacher induction practices in the district. When and if these measures passed, it would not be possible to disentangle the impact of DC VOICE's advocacy from the advocacy of other parties. At best, we could say whether the changes in policy were consistent with what DC VOICE advocated but not whether DC VOICE's efforts were responsible.

Data Sources

We collected the following data from each case-study site each year from 2004 to 2009.

Documents

We tracked major newspapers in each area to understand the social, political, and economic context surrounding the collaborative and different educational issues and initiatives under way, and collected plans, brochures, flyers, and other materials created and distributed by each collaborative. We also gathered district documents that described financial issues within the district, reform initiatives, and available funding streams.

Yearly Site Visits with Interviews, Focus Groups, and Informal Observations

Table 2.1 shows the number of interviews for each year of the project by site. The site visits in 2004, 2006, 2007, and 2009 included relatively large numbers of interviews. Teams of two to three RAND researchers spent approximately two to three days at each site. During site visits, we met individually with members of the collaborative to understand

Table 2.1
Number of Interviewees

Location	2004	2005	2006	2007	2008	2009	Total
Austin	26	4	24	15	4	19	92
Chicago	22	4	16	12	3	17	74
Jackson	21	7	14	17	2	17	78
Puerto Rico	38	5	5	25	17	N/A	90
Washington, D.C.	12	1	20	12	2	14	61
Total interviews	119	21	79	81	28	67	395

NOTE: We count only two people in each focus group even though there tended to be more. We found that, sometimes, interviewees came and left at different times for these groups, so we simply estimated the lowest number. Also, in 2005, we met only with the lead collaborative members.

the extent of each group's activities and how the Ford Foundation grant funding was being used. We specifically followed up with each grantee to determine what data it had collected to establish its impact according to the memoranda of understanding (MOUs).

In Puerto Rico and Jackson, where grantees had cluster-level activities, we visited schools in each cluster, usually two elementary schools, one middle school, and one high school. In each school, we interviewed the principal for approximately one hour about school climate, recent changes in the school, professional development, and community support. We interviewed teachers in groups of four to five. We interviewed school counselors and any other school personnel assisting with collaborative efforts.

At the district level, RAND staff interviewed selected school board members, the superintendent of schools, the director of testing and evaluation, and the district contact for the collaborative. Interviews with supervisors for professional development, feeder pattern planning (usually the assistant superintendent for curriculum and instruction), and the budget were also conducted.

Within the larger community, we interviewed or met with parent groups, contacts from churches, members of business partnerships, key politicians, and others who supported school reform and collaborative efforts. In some cases, the grantees had their own evaluators in place. We actively sought to discuss issues with these evaluators and understand their local evaluation efforts.

Site visits in 2005 and 2008 were more abbreviated. In 2005, the site visits consisted of the foundation program officer, the RAND team staff from LCN, and the sites' leaders. Together, in a large-group format, we established MOUs that detailed each grantee's specific intentions, what each hoped to accomplish by 2009, and how it would be determined whether progress had been made. The sites were responsible for collecting and providing these data.

In 2008, due to reduced resources, we used primarily phone calls to catch up with site leads, with the exception of Puerto Rico. This was its last year of the grant, and we completed a comprehensive visit that year and did not return in 2009.

A set of protocols was developed that was common across the sites but slightly different for each type of interviewee. For example, there were separate protocols for principals, superintendents, collaborative members, and foundations. At the same time, given the different intentions of each collaborative, a set of questions and probes unique to that collaborative was appended to the common protocol to ensure that we covered site-specific issues. In addition to the protocols, we had a list specific to each of the documents and evidence to be collected.

To the extent possible, we attempted to track progress of the unique initiatives specified by the grantees. Site visits were coordinated with important collaborative and school activities, such as parent-teacher association (PTA), school board, or town meetings, so that community members targeted by the collaborative could be interviewed and activities observed informally. (We did not have a specific protocol for observations but attended meetings to understand the types of issues collaboratives faced and how they acted to promote their goals.)

In most cases, a team of two RAND staff carried out the interviews: One conducted the interview while the other took notes. The team reviewed these notes for accuracy. They were later analyzed to develop yearly case-study reports provided to the sites for an accuracy check and to the foundation to ensure that it understood what progress was made during that yearly time frame.

The Urban Partnership Program and CERI 1 Phone Survey

In the final year of the study, we attempted to conduct phone interviews with members of all the former UPP grantees (N = 16) and the former CERI 1 grantees (N = 5 without double counting the three UPP sites that were later CERI sites) to determine whether partnerships were still in existence, what lessons had been learned about scale-up and sustainment of reform efforts, and what thoughts they had with regard to the usefulness of collaboration in promoting community reforms.

Administrative Data

With the help of key contacts in each school district, we gathered data on school demographic characteristics, school performance indicators, and community profiles to understand the changes in the school and communities that might affect the initiatives.

Analysis

The data collected were compiled on a yearly basis into an internal report for each grantee. Each site checked its report for facts prior to submittal to the foundation. The reports serve as the record of progress made, along with the documents and artifacts collected.

To determine what initiatives the collaborating groups chose to implement and whether these made sense (study questions 1a and 1b), we analyzed the interview and proposal information and any feedback from the grantees. We complemented this with specific reviews of the literature on those types of interventions—when a literature was available. Looking at both the site context, including specific needs identified and other initiatives under way, and the literature, we drew logical conclusions about the appropriateness of the interventions.

To assess whether sites showed progress toward the foundation's goals (question 1c), we created specific indicators from the literature (see "Literature Review" later in this chapter). We took the information from the case studies and, using the indicators, arrayed the activities across each site in summative form. We assigned a value to the activities in terms of the extent to which progress had been made. These were usually straightforward assessments as to whether site respondents described the activity as having no progress, being in the planning stages, being piloted or demonstrated, or being implemented across the set of agencies or providers as originally planned. Different types of indicators were used to describe the level of collaborative function (see "Indicators of Progress" later in this chapter).

The case-study data were then analyzed for cross-site patterns to address research question 2: whether lessons or promising practices could be drawn. Variation among the grantees provided us with the means to draw interesting contrasts that could help the field understand the conditions under which certain approaches were chosen and flourished. In addition, we reviewed the interviews for cross-site themes.

We briefed yearly findings to the foundation and the grantees, and the foundation used those findings to encourage progress or changes in emphasis. We then briefed the final findings to the foundation, and the foundation provided comments on the draft report.

Study Limitations

This analysis has an important caveat. Although the study followed the progress of the sites over multiple years, it relied heavily on evidence from the last set of interviews and reported future plans for determining the advancement of the collaborative efforts.

Literature Review

Two literatures seemed relevant to the Ford Foundation's initiative: the literature on collaboratives interested in improving social or education services, and the literature on implementation of education reforms. We reviewed these to help us develop useful expectations for progress and to define specific indicators of more-general concepts when possible. Much of the review provided here was first completed under the previous study (Bodilly, Chun, et al., 2004) and is paraphrased from that previous report. Some sections might appear similar to those of that report.

Interorganizational Linkages

We found the literature on interorganizational collaboration to support social and educational reforms consisted largely of case studies of existing or attempted collaboration. The case studies typically included qualitative descriptions of such collaborative efforts as school-community partnerships, teacher collaboratives, and partnerships between neighborhood and community-based organizations, to name a few. Specific expectations for progress or outcomes and empirical evidence of any outcomes produced by collaborative efforts were usually missing from these reports.

Hogue (1994), Keith (1993), Mattessich and Monsey (1992), Himmelman (1996), Lieberman and McLaughlin (1992), and Winer and Ray (1994) indicate several levels of interactions among organizations that we found useful for describing progress toward collaboration. Himmelman (1996), Hogue (1994), Keith (1993), and Lieberman and McLaughlin (1992) defined networking as the exchange of information for an individual's mutual benefit with flexible structure and with loosely defined roles for participants. Melaville and Blank (1991), Mattessich and Monsey (1992), Himmelman (1996), and Winer and Ray (1994) agreed that cooperation and coordination describe a set of interorganizational linkages that include short-term, jointly held goals in which organizational partners share information only about the subject at hand, with each organization retaining its mission, goals, and programs.

Melaville and Blank (1991) describe collaboration as the strongest form of interorganizational linkage, in which the partners establish common goals and pursue them with jointly sponsored activities:

> In order to address problems that lie beyond any single agency's exclusive purview, but which concern them all, partners agree to pool resources, jointly plan, implement, and evaluate new services and procedures, and delegate individual responsibility for the outcomes of their joint efforts. (p. 14)

Similarly, Wenger (1998) suggests that a "joint enterprise" is kept together by "joint work" with mutual and reciprocal accountability. By joining together, the partners increase their collective political clout to ensure more-comprehensive service delivery. Collaborations bring previously separate organizations into a joint structure with a common mission and are used when the need and intent are to fundamentally change the way in which services are designed and delivered (Melaville and Blank, 1991). The benefits of collaborative approaches are efficiency in provision of resources, individual efficacy for members, and integration of expertise and resources. Among the challenges are the need for inclusive leadership that promotes effective participation by relevant stakeholders, the ability to make sufficient time for relationships to develop, the difficulty of balancing risk and benefits among partners, the difficulty of building and reinforcing structural and institutional supports, and a failure to agree on basic goals and approaches (Keith, 1993; Kaganoff, 1998; Himmelman, 1996; Iwanowsky, 1996; Baker, 1993). Strong past relationships among the community organizations, agreement on the problem to be addressed, and adequate resources to implement the solutions all play a positive role in encouraging a collaborative's progress toward its goals. The experiences of CERI 1 reinforce these findings (Bodily, Chun, et al., 2004).

Expectations for Implementation

Changing the behaviors of staff in existing organizations is difficult and further complicated by the multiple levels of government involved in schooling. It is made even more difficult when significantly different behaviors are called for, the tasks and behaviors are those of a large and diverse group, and the targeted groups have varying incentives to change (Mazmanian and Sabatier, 1989)—all conditions that hold for schools (Gitlin and Margonis, 1995; Cuban, 1984; Huberman and Miles, 1984).

Attempts at implementation of specific interventions aimed at teaching lead to changes in behaviors in significant but nonuniform and unexpected ways (Berman et al., 1975). Adaptation sometimes leads to less-benign effects, such as disappearance, erosion, dilution, drift, or simply slowed implementation (Cuban, 1984; Pressman and Wildavsky, 1973; Daft, 1982; Mazmanian and Sabatier, 1989; McDonnell and Grubb, 1991: Weatherley and Lipsky, 1977; Yin, 1979). These types of outcomes should be expected if the collaboratives failed to foster good will with policymakers, the community did not have the social or intellectual capacity to support the desired changes or the infusion of resources in terms of time, funding, and information—referred to as slack or slack resources—were not made available. The education literature points to important supports that can lead to implementation closer to that desired, such as funding, professional development resources, and active participation of the leadership (McLaughlin, 1990).

Finally, the foundation's growing interest in community organizing to develop a voice for education reform was informed by several authors (Shirley, 1997; Warren, 2001). This literature provides case studies of local efforts by CBOs to affect policy. Its innovation is to "reground politics in community institutions and their values as a way to reinvigorate political participation of public leadership" (Warren, 2001, p. 242). It emphasizes that organizers involve multiple constituencies and use negotiation to affect policy. As Shirley (1997, p. 284) states,

> Most educators and school reformers try to keep politics out of discussions about schools—as [if] that were possible or desirable in a robust democracy. The Alliance Schools take an altogether different stance, and suggest that educators and reformers can better serve urban children and their parents if they frankly recognize the interplay between politics and education in the public schools and consciously endeavor to appeal to constituencies which cross lines of race, class and religion.

This literature does not provide specific principles to judge effectiveness but, consistent with the literature on collaboration and education implementation, notes the importance of local conditions in determining an agenda and the important role of leadership in organizing.[1]

Implications

Based on its convictions and experiences with the UPP sites, the foundation staff hoped that collaboration among the different local agencies and CBOs would bring about coherence instead of the more-normal fragmentation. We note that the available literature does not provide evidence that this would, in fact, be the case. Rather, as noted, the literature on education reform pointed to significant challenges for any attempts at reform.

From the foundation staff's point of view, a characteristic of success for the initiative, therefore, would be whether the collaborative could encourage changes in policies to make them more supportive of improved teaching and learning. Another was whether the col-

---

[1] At the beginning of CERI, there was very little literature in this area of community organizing for education reform. It has grown somewhat since then.

laborative gained stature or "voice" in the community such that it brought different CBOs together to work more effectively to ensure supportive policy or to participate in governing structures that made more-coherent policy—especially, according to the foundation staff, on behalf of those who were formerly underrepresented in education decisionmaking or underserved by current policies. In this regard, the foundation staff wanted a special focus on those who were formerly underrepresented in education decisionmaking or underserved by current policies.

Importantly, the foundation did not prescribe a set of interventions; these were to be developed by the collaboratives. And the collaboratives each had different starting places and contexts—and, therefore, different appropriate interventions, as well as starting points in terms of local will and capacity. Given these differences, we would expect significant variation among the sites in terms of both starting points and progress.

The literature suggests several other considerations when assessing progress:

- Collaborative efforts are challenging and often develop slowly and unevenly, if at all.
- Partners might arrive at different levels of interorganizational linkages due to leadership actions to promote or inhibit collaborative functions and involve relevant stakeholders.
- Collaboration as the mechanism to encourage change requires new behaviors among the partners, as well as new behaviors by teachers, school personnel, parents, and district managers.
- Contextual factors are expected to strongly affect whether a collaborative's history, existing community understanding and agreement about the problem and need for comprehensive solutions, and adequate resources—including human—are likely to be associated with progress.
- Actual implementation of the collaborative strategies and plans should be expected to vary.

Indicators of Progress

In assessing progress, we used the expectation areas developed under CERI 1 and the same general level of progress (Bodily, Chun, et al., 2004). The areas are

- the level of development of interorganizational linkages or collaborative function and financial sustainability
- the level of development and implementation of plans for improving the quality of teaching and learning
- the level of development and implementation of plans for systemic changes in policy
- the level of development of a unique voice in the community that represents a constituency outside of the central office.

For the first of these, level of development of the interorganizational linkages, we used the slightly modified attributes, taken from the literature, that were strong indicators of collaborative function in CERI 1:

- It represented a broad group of stakeholders: The composition of partnerships was logical to all involved and included relevant stakeholders.
- It had inclusive leadership and effective decisionmaking structures: Decisionmaking structures and leadership encouraged joint decisionmaking, joint actions, and authentic collaborative interactions, regardless of the formal governance structure.
- It created shared goals among a group of partners: Collaborative members expressed strong buy-in to the goals of the collaborative.
- It created shared data and used data for decisionmaking: Members jointly collected and reviewed data on a regular basis, sharing information among members to form cohesion of purpose, improve decisionmaking, and coordinate actions.
- It shared information broadly: The collaborative jointly provided information to stakeholders to influence public decisions, including mounting public information campaigns.

- It developed stable sources of funding and pooling of resources: Organizations combined resources (foundation funding, personnel time, and other sources of funding) to pursue the collaborative mission, as opposed to funneling foundation grants to the members to fund their individual operations. In addition, they created and pursued successfully strategies to find stable and sustained funding.[2]
- It implemented coordinated or joint actions and developed joint products: Organizations developed activities together and implemented them jointly (as opposed to implementing the existing activities of each partner in parallel or with some level of coordination) and held each other accountable for the outcomes. Joint actions led to joint products of the members—clearly labeled as from the group, not the individual members.

We assessed the level of progress using the three levels indicated in the literature—networking, coordinating, and collaborating—based on what was evident at the last set of interviews and in plans at that point. By the last of our site visits, some partners were accomplishing little more than network-level information sharing. And even though they might have reached greater levels of collaboration in the past, if they did not have evidence of concrete plans with funding for more collaborative activities, we labeled them as currently (as of spring 2009) functioning at lower levels of interorganizational linkages. Those grantees whose partners were working to coordinate some of the above activities, we considered coordinating partners. Those that were involved in the full set of the above activities with solid plans for more of that type of work, we labeled collaboratives. In Chapter Three, we assess progress on each of these indicators. We also provide our intuitive assess-

---

[2] In addition, the foundation expected the grantees to eventually become independent of the need for foundation funds. In part, this is a common expectation of foundations that do not wish to be seen as permanently attached to a site. Independence can also be seen as a sign that the collaborative has become successful. It might imply that the collaborative has grown to the point that it is fully functioning as a private nonprofit, that it is able to charge fees for its work, or that other groups or funders find the activities so compelling that they provide further support.

ment of the trajectory for collaboration for each site, based on the final set of interviews and reviews of future plans and access to sustaining funds. This is not based on a numerical calculation but on a comparative assessment against the above set of activities. The accuracy of the trajectory assessment should be quite clear given the evidence.

For the other three areas listed above, we used a common system for assessing progress developed in Bodilly, Keltner, et al. (1998). Progress can be seen for any specific activity as being at one of three levels:

- Not accomplished: activities that were described in documents or in interviews as planned to be undertaken or as not undertaken or for which the sites provided evidence that little or no progress was made.
- Partially accomplished: sets of activities that were described in documents or in interviews as having been undertaken and with some partial progress having been made. For example, a program that was supposed to be developed, tested in a demonstration, and then extended throughout the district was developed but extended to only a handful of other schools.
- Accomplished: Planned activities were accomplished in a fashion that closely resembled what was planned as described in documents and interviews.

CHAPTER THREE

Progress Toward Collaborative Functioning and Sustainment

In this chapter, we describe the attempts at collaborative formation, assess the extent to which the grantees developed fully functioning interorganizational collaboratives and sustained funding as expressed in research question 1a, and draw lessons relevant to the formation of the collaboratives in response to research question 2. When describing progress, we focus particularly on two of the progress indicators for the foundation's goals for its effort: the level of development of interorganizational linkages or collaborative function and the level of financial sustainability achieved by the grantee.

The chapter presents an overview of our assessment of the progress made and then describes each grantee's effort and status in more detail. We include information about whether the grantees were able to create a sustainable funding stream for the work of the collaborative. Included after this assessment is a short review of what happened to the original UPP and CERI 1 sites in terms of whether they managed to sustain themselves. We end with themes drawn from a cross-case analysis.

Overview of Progress Toward Collaborative Function and Sustainment

Using the indicators discussed in Chapter Two, we assessed the progress made for each grantee toward full collaborative function. We especially depended on the set of activities that were noted in the literature as important in collaborative work: representing a broad group of stakeholders and being inclusive, using data for decisionmaking and sharing information widely, having shared goals and implementing joint and coordinated actions, and gaining a stable funding base and pooling resources, which we consider to be the same as the Ford goal of creating a sustained funding source.

Our assessment of these factors in the spring of 2009 is summarized in Table 3.1. Overall, the data indicate that one of the grantees ended CERI 2 as a fully functioning collaborative with relatively sustainable sources of funding (AI). The Alianza faltered, having few viable collaborative activities planned as of the last visit in 2008. The remaining three retained interorganizational linkages among the partner organizations. The partners in these locations appeared to be rethinking their shared goals and joint activities in part due to the difficulty of gaining funding and the changing landscape of reform in their cities. In particular, we note the following:

- The Alianza in Puerto Rico (in 2008, at the end of the grant) had focused on creating the policy institute but lacked collaborative strength or funding to maintain or grow institute activities. Institute staff had been reduced, and the former Alianza partners were no longer meeting regularly while each pursued their own activities. The partners remained part of a network of organizations that shared information and general goals of improving education in Puerto Rico.

- The AFM collaborative in Jackson had left many of its original partners behind while PPS and the principals in the Lanier feeder pattern continued their work at a reduced level. PPS had transformed into an entity that still heavily used collaborative processes, but it had turned its attention to increasing arts-integration schools across Jackson under a separate Ford Foundation grant. AFM Arts was a collaborative with schools and principals across Jackson, including those in the Lanier pattern. The principals in the Lanier feeder pattern that were the focus of the CERI effort still maintained strong collaborative ties with each other but no longer had the financial support needed to carry on their joint work in as vigorous a fashion.

Table 3.1
Sites' Progress Toward Attaining and Growing Collaboration (2009)

Progress Indicator	The Alianza	AFM	AI	DC VOICE	GYO
Represented broad group of stakeholders	No new stakeholders; original partners drifted away	Original partners drifted away; PPS began leading effort at arts integration with new partners	Had growing set of partners for new initiatives that represent diverse interests	Represented parents and voters; was partnering with other organizations on specific issues	Member organizations represented diverse groups and added new partners as expanded
Had inclusive leadership and effective decisionmaking	Provided policy forums	No growth or outreach outside of arts; principals' council continued to use inclusive decisionmaking	Continued to build through forums; used community organizing; used public stakeholder voting	Became a single entity and sought partner on specific issues based on value added	Was inclusive among original partners but not always among program consortium members
Created shared goals among a group of partners	Partners no longer met regularly to pursue shared goals	Had built over time, but PPS began to focus on arts while others focused on different areas	Maintained pipeline-shared goals; was building partnerships on specific goals through forums	Shared goals with specific partners on specific issues	Original partners were dedicated to GYO
Created shared data and used data for decisionmaking	No funds for data gathering	Provided professional development on data-driven decisionmaking to schools but was no longer active	Included as part of process	Developed data through community research	Developed and used in original program development; inconsistent later

Table 3.1—Continued

Progress Indicator	The Alianza	AFM	AI	DC VOICE	GYO
Shared information broadly	Dismissed with lack of funds	Was major function with significant sharing among schools and parents; had begun to diminish	Shared broadly with all partners and stakeholders	Major emphasis was to get information to public through, e.g., town hall meetings, consumer newsletters, testimony, and press	Selected specific information to publicize
Implemented coordinated joint actions and developed joint products	After initial years, stopped joint actions	Remained active on arts	Worked with partners to influence legislation and policy	Jointly carried out specific issue-area campaigns	Routinely coordinated to implement GYO
Developed stable funding sources and pooling of resources	None	None for broader efforts of the past	Yes, through church members and grants	Multiple grants	Dependent on annual state allocation for GYO
Trajectory of collaboration— overall assessment	Network still functioned to share information, but no specific shared goals or ongoing activities	Declining coordination; PPS was searching for funding for process of collaboration to enable further reform	Had growing collaborative and coordination efforts; static on pipeline but was increasing linkages and collaborative efforts for policy issues	Moved from collaborative to single CBO that coordinated with specific organizations on specific short-term issues of interest	Static coordination; organizations coordinated on pipeline program implementation; networked and coordinated as other interests aligned

- Although grant funding remains uncertain in the recessionary environment, AI created and sustained a collaborative of churches and other interested groups dedicated to sustained reform in general and focused on the south Austin neighborhood schools in particular. Its efforts were flourishing at the time of our visit and had policy impact at the state level. Because the collaborative relies at least in part on contributions from the church members in the form of funding and volunteer time, it appeared to have some wherewithal to survive an economic downturn.
- DC VOICE became a 501(c)(3) in its own right and no longer functioned as an interorganizational collaborative, although it maintained important partnerships on specific issue areas and had successfully sought out new funding for its efforts.
- GYO in Chicago used collaborative means to ensure passage of a state-funded teacher pipeline program (funded annually by state appropriations). The original organizations each had a role to play as contractors or subcontractors to the state in this new program and continued to meet to implement the program as contractors. They were considering expansion of the pipeline to include mentoring and induction components. The original organizations in varying combinations still worked together on new initiatives but were functioning more as an ongoing network with strong prior ties from their successful efforts and occasional partners on specific activities.

The Alianza, Puerto Rico

The Alianza was formed through a Ford Foundation UPP planning grant in 1994 with the vision of proving that, as described by an Alianza leader, "in low-performing schools and districts with the worst socioeconomic conditions, it was possible to establish education reform, foster environments of change, and promote new cultures of education." In 1998, when the UPP initiative ended, the foundation invited the Alianza Metropolitana de San Juan Para La Educación to apply for a CERI grant. The Alianza proposed to apply lessons learned from the UPP initiative to 11 schools in the Cataño district, which would act as an educational laboratory to demonstrate better practices to schools throughout the island. The College Board, Sacred Heart University, the Puerto Rico Community Foundation, and Aspira partnered to form the Alianza. Cataño schools agreed to be a laboratory for testing new educational strategies and vision.

For the next several years, the group built a collaborative effort and successfully introduced new practices into the schools in Cataño. The evaluation of the first phase of CERI gave the collaborative high marks for working together effectively. The activities included a collective mission and vision exercise for development of a strategic plan for improvement; promoting and developing individualized student pedagogy; considerable professional development, including trips to observe high-performing schools in Puerto Rico; and the development of Spanish-language counseling protocols and student aspiration surveys.

The progress made was judged to be successful enough for the Alianza to receive additional funds from the Kellogg Foundation to scale up the Cataño work in five other districts in Puerto Rico under a project called Demonstrative District for the Systemic Change in Education (DECCES). The activities fostered in the original Cataño schools began to spread to these five districts.

For CERI 2 in 2004, the Alianza outlined objectives to institutionalize its progress, including creating a laboratory for systemic educational change; creating a center for capacity building and dissemination; and creating the Institute of Educational Policy for Community Development (IPEDCo). In 2005, IPEDCo was formally established as a part of the Alianza, with the objective of researching effective education initiatives and making education policy recommendations. And in 2007, the Secretary of Education in Puerto Rico announced that the department would adopt the Alianza's systemic-change model as a guide for transforming schools in the future. The secretary met with the foundation to explain his intentions.

With this added mission, but facing dwindling funds as the Kellogg funding came to an end, the new Alianza strategy included ending the current model of DECCES services in the districts by 2007. In 2006, planning shifted to consolidate the Laboratory for Systemic

Educational Change and the Center for Capacity Building and Dissemination into one body, IPEDCo, to be governed by the Alianza. IPEDCo planned to have a technical assistance unit that would offer a catalog of services to schools and districts on a fee-for-service basis, similar to those offered in the Alianza model. Fees generated would sustain IPEDCo research. Additional foundation-provided revenue was set aside with the Puerto Rico Community Foundation (PRCF) to fund IPEDCo, assuming that it could produce a viable plan.

In 2008, IPEDCo leaders met with the Secretary of Education once again to notify him of the end of the Alianza and the new IPEDCo focus. The secretary encouraged IPEDCO to take on a major research project into the nature, functions, and limits of the school district in Puerto Rico. In December 2008, IPEDCo presented a preliminary report to the secretary, but there had been no follow-up at the time of our visit.[1]

Economic turmoil took over Puerto Rico starting in 2006 and grew throughout this time period. Unrest in the education sector was exacerbated by political scandals in the governor's office. The partners drifted apart as each strove to survive in the difficult environment with cuts in education budgets, scandals in commonwealth government, and shrinking foundation assets focused on education.

The leadership of IPEDCo changed several times during this period. The leader of the collaborative in Puerto Rico in the days of the UPP was a charismatic and well-known educational reform figure in the island—a professor from the Sacred Heart University. He was an expert at collaboration and building a vision of child-centered pedagogy. He could speak both humbly and passionately about what improved pedagogy might do for the children of the island. During CERI 1, he stepped down and was replaced by his protégé, also a well-known professor at the university. She carried the imprimatur of the original leader, and, in fact, he still came to meetings and helped to build morale around the vision through his speeches. But, with a change in the political party in power, she left for a high-level position in government.

---

[1] By 2009, however, a new party was in power and a new secretary had taken over.

She was replaced by a succession of two less-well-known professors from the university. From 2007 to 2009, with dwindling funds and seriously dwindling staff, these leaders focused on completing the policy research on the district strategy in Puerto Rico and held forums urging reform. Respondents noted that, during this stressful time, IPEDCo was not associated with any changes to policies and did not gain any new funding, from PRCF or others.

At the time of our last visit in 2008, the original organizations involved reported that they were no longer working closely together or meeting regularly but could be said to be a part of a network of organizations still interested in reform. The IPEDCo leaders did not articulate any further plans for IPEDCo. Rather, they and others reported that the president of the university was trying to gather education policy actors together in a meeting to help determine what IPEDCo's future might be.

Ask for More, Jackson, Mississippi

In 1998, Jackson had a large low-income population and little prospect for economic growth in the surrounding economy, and Jackson Public Schools (JPS) served a declining student population. JPS had experienced very high turnover in district leadership, with four superintendents in the five years prior to CERI 1. During the initiative, the rate of turnover slowed significantly.

Jackson received a one-year planning grant for $100,000 in 1998 and was selected in August 1999 by the Ford Foundation to receive an implementation grant of about $300,000 per year throughout the CERI 1 efforts. PPS was the lead organization in creating the collaborative, with JPS, Mississippi Human Services Agenda, Millsaps College, Public Education Forum, and the Southern Initiative of the Algebra Project as members. The collaborative named itself *Ask for More* and focused on the Lanier feeder pattern, which served approximately 4,800 students in the poorest section of the district. The AMF collaborative focused initially on providing supports to schools for improvement and on the development of principals within the cluster. Millsaps

College offered training for principals, and the AFM principals began attending each summer.

After a series of early missteps, in 2000, the AFM collaborative reorganized itself under the leadership of a new head of PPS. Prior to that time, only the lead principals in the feeder pattern were included in the collaborative meeting. After holding a meeting with several key representatives, the group decided that all principals would be actively engaged as partners in the collaborative. The Principal's Council became the lead in terms of moving the effort forward, while PPS kept responsibility as the fiduciary agent, major convener, and support provider of the principal-based collaborative. Other member organizations provided support and services for the principals' efforts to improve teaching and learning within the feeder pattern (see Bodilly, Chun, et al., 2004, for details).

In 2004, with the continuing funding from the Ford Foundation for CERI 2, AFM continued down the same pathway with a few changes. First, over time, the original partners dropped out—only PPS and the Lanier-feeder-pattern principals remained involved with the initiative by the spring of 2009. Meanwhile, the idea of collaboration across the schools in the feeder pattern spread to include cross-school collaboration by teachers and counselors. Other, less-central organizations came and went as priorities and interventions shifted.

Principals turned over in the Lanier feeder pattern throughout the study. Of the original ten principals from the feeder pattern involved in the collaborative, only two remained by 2009. Participants in AFM usually described this turnover in positive terms. First, AFM and PPS representatives were invited to interview candidates for a new principal position in the Lanier cluster to ensure that they were good fits for the collaborative work taking place. Second, many of the principals from the feeder pattern left for jobs at the central office. From their new positions, these principals assisted in scaling up ideas developed by AFM into the other feeder patterns within the district. For example, in 2007, one Lanier-feeder-pattern principal was promoted to assistant superintendent at JPS, and another became deputy superintendent for curriculum and instruction. The senior counselor at the high school was promoted to a district position in charge of student services with the added responsibility of overseeing the work of counselors across the district.

In the earlier years of AFM, leaders of the collaborative met together about once a month after a separate meeting of the Principal's Council. As the years wore on, the collaborative leadership group began meeting every other month, then less. By 2009, AFM no longer met separately in a leadership meeting. Instead, the Principal's Council continued on a monthly basis with the addition of PPS representatives attending as part of the meeting agenda.

In 2009, decisionmaking still resided with the principals through a consensus process. A major role of PPS was to work with JPS to provide detailed achievement data and guide principals and other school leaders through a review of the data and their implications for school improvement. Information was shared through meetings, and, over time, much information sharing began to take place electronically. At the time of our last visit, the principals and PPS actively shared information on a multitude of factors—anything from the school schedule to school counselors across the grade levels meeting before the beginning of the school year to exchange information about specific students. School counselors also met throughout the year to plan, discuss, and implement strategies and eventually produced a counselor's guide for AFM.

With CERI 2, however, PPS's attention began to focus more heavily on a new Ford Foundation–funded arts initiative. The arts-integration initiative involved some of the Lanier feeder schools but also other schools, and it adopted collaborative processes. In interviews during our last site visit in 2009, a number of parents and school staff could not distinguish between AFM and AFM Arts (the name of this new initiative).

By this time, the collaborative had become more of a partnership between two entities: PPS and the Lanier-feeder-pattern principals. PPS offered limited support to the schools as funding dwindled. Furthermore, PPS's ability to sustain reform in the feeder schools became more difficult as leadership within the district turned over in favor of a superintendent and board that collaborative members reported as being interested in micromanaging the schools from the central office.

In addition, several public scandals associated with city and district leadership rocked the community and disrupted improvement efforts.

By 2009, financial sustainment of the AFM collaborative was uncertain, as was its influence with the superintendent and board. PPS had already switched its attention to integration of the arts and other initiatives but was searching for funding sources other than the Ford Foundation. In addition, new board members and the superintendent were no longer interested in collaborative activities and had begun new initiatives of their own. Leaders of PPS continued to advocate for changes and encourage a strong voice at community forums but were frustrated that this newfound voice might be falling on deaf ears.

In 2009, some sources in Jackson argued that the collaborative, as defined under CERI, was no longer necessary precisely because AFM had been successful. They had built a strong Principal's Council in the Lanier feeder pattern, and certain interventions that started in the cluster had moved on to gain district support. As one respondent put it,

> There has been capacity building over these ten years for everyone. For PPS, for Jackson Public Schools as a district, and individual schools, too, there was a huge void at the beginning in this community's capacity to collaborate. They couldn't do it at the beginning. And AFM has become the people they look to.

In short, the collaborative processes built over time by PPS and the Lanier principals took hold and were successfully scaled up to other feeder patterns and even to the district offices through promotion of Lanier principals. But the AFM collaborative itself had become a partnership with few resources left to provide support for school improvement.

Austin Interfaith, Austin, Texas

The Austin collaborative was formed through a Ford Foundation CERI 2 grant in 2003. Prior to the grant, the lead collaborative organization, AI, headed the Alliance School Initiative. This initiative was designed to change the culture of schools in the Austin Independent

School District (AISD) and improve the quality of education through community organizing and the development of transformational parental engagement. It is this work that had come to the attention of the Ford Foundation when it encouraged AI to apply for the CERI grant.

With the Ford Foundation providing proposal-development funds, AI brought together a group of community representatives (e.g., parents, teachers, students) and institutional leaders from AISD, Education Austin (the teachers' association), and St. Edward's University to discuss the goals and actions that should be addressed in the proposal. At the time, AISD schools were facing a series of problems, including low performance, shortage of qualified teachers, and high teacher turnover. Five research action groups were formed and met regularly over the course of several months to review research and to discuss and identify ways to improve public schools in Austin. In light of their findings, they agreed on several goals that formed the basis of the proposal submitted to Ford. Two main goals included the creation of a pipeline of quality teachers and the expansion of the Alliance School Initiative, emphasizing a feeder-pattern approach.

Once funded, however, the five research groups held fewer meetings, and attention was focused on only one of the goals—the development of a pipeline of high-quality teachers. This emphasis resulted in adding two other collaborative members: Capital IDEA (an adult vocational training corporation) and Austin Community College.

Initially, the collaborating organizations varied in their vision of the pipeline and the population it should target. Each organization had a unique mission that needed to be consolidated with the collaborative mission. Although all agreed that a teacher pipeline was needed to address teacher quality and retention issues, the organizations had particular foci for their work. AI, whose work focused on improving the livelihood of the poor, envisioned the pipeline to target marginalized community members, such as paraprofessionals working in AISD schools in order to provide them with opportunities to become teachers and increase their wages. The colleges, whose goal was to address teacher shortages in eight different counties, envisioned the pipeline to embrace additional populations interested in teaching, including high school and community college students. This tension between AI and the colleges, however, lessened in subsequent years, as the colleges developed their own pipeline independent of the collaborative's efforts. This other effort targeted a wider population while continuing the colleges' commitment to the pipeline originally envisioned by AI.

Over the remaining years of CERI, the collaborative members strengthened their interactions over the pipeline. They expanded their membership to include Huston-Tillotson University as their pipeline evolved to address different specializations. The collaborative organizations met monthly as a group and more frequently to discuss specific tasks. They worked together to write accreditation agreements between community and four-year colleges and combined resources to support the pipeline efforts. For example, the four-year colleges provided scholarships and tuition reduction for pipeline candidates, while Capital IDEA provided them with the wrap-around services. AISD provided candidates with release time so they were able to attend classes. Additionally, the collaborative was successful in getting modest awards from various foundations and the city of Austin to continue with the pipeline. These awards provided adequate funds to ensure the support for the current group of teacher candidates throughout their program duration. However, there were no reports of additional funds for the pipeline in 2009. Without the provision of additional funds, it would be difficult to further expand the teacher pipeline and recruit additional teacher candidates.

AI expanded its vision to reemphasize the Alliance School Initiative when its leadership changed in 2007. The new leader thought that school improvement could not be accomplished without influencing both local and state policies, especially in relation to advocating for changes in student assessment and state accountability systems. In the following years, AI returned to its community-mobilizing mission to support advocacy for changes in state and local policies. AI partnered with local and state organizations. At the local level, AI reestablished its roots and connections to 25 congregations. In the following two years, these affiliations strengthened AI's mobilization efforts and provided continuous sources of funding through membership fees. During this time period, AI also reached out for the first time to business associations, such as the chamber of commerce, to identify the type of knowledge and skills needed for the Austin economy in order to inform the design of student assessment and accountability systems. At the state level, AI worked closely with sister organizations and the unions to exert pressure on state legislators. AI ran summits and forums at both the local and state levels to share information and research with a wide range of stakeholders on the effects of the state's accountability system and high-stakes testing. These summits and forums resulted in mobilizing the public to vote on these issues and in increased public commitment and funding.

DC VOICE, District of Columbia

Prior to the Ford Foundation's CERI 1, the CBO education sector in the District of Columbia was populated with significant numbers of small organizations, each promoting its own agenda and with little history of cooperation with each other. The schools were in poor shape, with falling enrollments and very poor performance. The school district as a whole appeared to be in a state of permanent crisis and was then under the purview of the U.S. government's Financial Control Board.

With a Ford Foundation planning grant in 1998, a group of CBOs, teachers, and parents were convened to discuss what could be done to bring about sustained improvements in the schools. These discussions occurred over several months, sometimes including workshops and seminars. The group applied for and was awarded implementation funding in 1999. The group called itself DC VOICE and was originally structured as an organization of individuals who were often affiliated with CBOs, and with Network of Educators on the Americas as the fiduciary agent. Originally, it focused considerable attention on providing professional development and other services and supports to specific neighborhood schools. Many respondents saw the CERI grant as a chance to build a fully functioning local education fund and to unite the many fragmented community-based education organizations in the district.

In 2003, DC VOICE responded to the CERI 2 request for proposals (RFP) with a clarified mission to ensure that every child in
the district had a high-quality public education. Upon receiving the
grant, it began to focus its efforts on affecting policy—specifically, by
(1) building a broad-based, well-informed public to take collaborative
action, (2) developing supports for expansion of effective local practices, and (3) acting as a catalyst for local policy changes around Supports for Quality Teaching (SQT). As part of this effort, it developed
the Ready Schools Project, a community-based research project that
reports publicly how ready the schools are to open each year.

In 2004, the individual membership model changed into a
501(c)(3) nonprofit organization, with a staff, a board, a steering committee, and several issue-specific committees representing various
CBOs. This led to the overhaul of the collaborative's governance and
committee structure, which had remained fairly stable since that time,
with the exception of changes in leadership in 2007 that brought new
direction.

Under the new leadership, the collaborative became an organization that partnered with other organizations or individuals on thematic
issues, such as ensuring that all schools were fully staffed and had the
supplies needed by the first day of school. It received grants from other
agencies, including the Public Education Network (PEN). The PEN
grant helped enable it to become a local education fund.

In 2007, the mayoral takeover of the D.C. public schools, together
with leadership changes, led DC VOICE to reexamine its trajectory. As
one respondent put it, "the mayoral takeover of 2007 probably helped
create a pause in our policy work as we and our partners have all struggled to identify just what each new entity does and what it has responsibility for."

In 2008, DC VOICE decided to expand its vision to include
community mobilizing and to become more strategic in selecting its
partner organizations. Although DC VOICE used collaborative mechanisms, it was best described as a CBO with strong partners on specific
issues rather than as a collaborative. It saw its goals as educating the
public to be more collaborative and to support reform efforts in the
district through community-based research and community mobiliz-

ing. It was directed by the board and no longer needed to reach organizational consensus in its decisionmaking. The new leader was adept at pursuing funding from other foundations for specific projects, and he had staffed the board to help ensure funding into the future.

For example, in 2009, the Ready Schools Project received funding from sources other than the Ford Foundation, and DC VOICE was publishing the Ready Schools report on a regular basis. It also presented objective findings to the city council and published newsletters, flyers, and email alerts on issues to a large distribution list of policymakers, community members, and interested education observers in the district. It also produced a report with others on the state of District of Columbia Public Schools (DCPS) school facilities. It partnered with other organizations on specific issues as the need arose.

In the end, the foundation had helped launch a new organization that pursued partnerships with other CBOs, but there was no longer a functioning collaborative.

Grow Your Own, Chicago, Illinois

Chicago has a long history of educational reform activities. Long before CERI, the efforts by CBOs in Chicago had resulted in school improvement and legislative changes. However, schools in low-income areas continued to underperform and experience high teacher turnover and shortage of high-quality teachers.

In 2001, the Association of Community Organizations for Reform Now (ACORN) approached the Ford Foundation about funding for its own work pertaining to educational reform. The foundation encouraged ACORN to apply for funding but suggested that it include a diverse group of CBOs in its efforts. It specifically named Design for Change (DFC), which had been credited with the passage of a major school-reform bill in Chicago. ACORN considered a variety of partners and decided to collaborate with organizations with which it had some history of cooperation. These organizations included DFC, the Logan Square Neighborhood Association (LSNA), and the Cross City Campaign for Urban School Reform (CCC).

In 2002, the foundation awarded the four organizations a year-long planning grant. Leaders from each of the four organizations met at least five times during the planning year, along with invited representatives from other institutions. In these meetings, participants reviewed data and discussed issues that the Chicago Public Schools (CPS) faced. The group reached consensus on what goals would become the focus of the collaborative. The goals included (1) the implementation of strategies to improve teaching in low-income areas; (2) the development of a teacher pipeline designed to recruit and train individuals with close ties to communities with hard-to-staff schools; and (3) strengthening the collaboration among member organizations.

The proposal was funded in 2003, and joint work and continued discussion focused on the creation of the teacher pipeline. Collaborating organizations agreed to pursue formal state legislation to create the pipeline—a strategy that could ensure sustained funding and potentially provide sufficient numbers of teachers to reduce teacher shortages and turnover, as well as to promote community economic development. Initially, decisions were made by consensus, and all voices held equal weight. Partners contributed differently but each in a substantial way. For example, ACORN organized communities and constituencies to support the pipeline idea, while DFC analyzed research about other GYO programs and shared this information with partners. CCC convened meetings and produced strategic and action-oriented publications, research, and tools.

However, within a year of receiving the CERI 2 grant, communication and trust with one specific collaborative organization deteriorated, as a result of disagreements over the nature of legislation and perceived unilateral actions without proper consultation. The disagreements primarily stemmed from the divergence of organizations' missions, specifically in relation to the neighborhood groups the pipeline would serve. The collaborative drafted and submitted a bill; without informing the others, DFC drafted and submitted a competing bill. In 2004, the bill drafted by the collaborative members passed and was signed into law as the GYO initiative. The GYO initiative demonstrated the CBOs' collaborative power in accomplishing a quick legislative win through advocacy, lobbying activities, and coalition building.

Although initial efforts were made to reunite the members, eventually, the others asked DFC to stop participating in the collaborative's efforts.

In 2005 and 2006, the collaborative extended its membership to four new CBOs: TARGET Area, Kenwood Oakland Community Organization, Southwest Organizing Project, and Little Village Community Development Corporation (LVCDC). CCC went out of business and therefore was no longer part of the collaborative. The four new organizations were already established, were connected within their communities, and had a history of improving neighborhood schools through policy action. Their involvement increased the collaborative's political power at both the local and state levels and strengthened its connections to both the African American and Hispanic communities in Chicago.

All six organizations shared similar visions and continued to focus their efforts on implementing the GYO initiative. The partners shared necessary information with one another, committed resources, and engaged in joint decisionmaking. Collaborative members met formally at least once a month and worked together more frequently to lobby state policymakers to ensure that the legislature would pass the GYO appropriation. However, the collaborative needed to make its case to the state each year to receive funds.

The law made provision for consortia in communities statewide to build the pipeline, and GYO did research to determine the need in different communities. It supported the organization of consortia in high-need areas, including Chicago. The state used an RFP process to fund consortia, which were to include a CBO, a two-year college and a four-year college, and a school district or group of schools. Each of the six organizations in the collaborative applied for consortium funding to establish a GYO initiative in its community. The organizations also won a competitive RFP to provide technical assistance to consortia statewide to set up the pipelines. GYO was awarded the technical-assistance contract, and all of the partner organizations successfully competed to create consortia in their Chicago neighborhoods. Therefore, the collaborative, as well as its members, became implementation contractors to the state. They have been successful in receiving state funds on an annual basis since fiscal year (FY) 2006 to implement GYO and to provide technical assistance to other GYO initiatives across the state. However, in later years, the collaborative did not receive the full amount requested. This hindered the collaborative's effort to expand the pipeline and to meet its goals of recruiting 1,000 teacher candidates by 2016.

By spring 2009, 16 consortia statewide were actively implementing the GYO pipeline. Seven of the eight consortia in Chicago were led by members of the collaborative.

The formation of the consortia forged additional linkages between collaborative member organizations, community colleges, four-year universities, and CPS. The relationships that developed between CBOs and the two- and four-year colleges were not always collaborative in nature, partly due to differences in the missions, culture, and operations between the two types of organizations. In some consortia, the GYO activities were poorly coordinated. The higher-education institutions were sometimes excluded from major decisions or discussions pertaining to the GYO efforts. For example, the CBOs exerted pressure on the universities to modify their curricula to include community organizing, without engaging them in open discussion. In addition to CBOs' hegemony in the decision structure, some colleges complained that CBOs lacked an understanding of practical and cost issues that the universities faced to meet the needs of teacher candidates. Shortly after our visit, however, the collaborative formed a formal decision-making body (the GYO Partners Council) that included consortium partners, reportedly to ensure greater inclusiveness in decisionmaking.

From 2007 to 2009, the collaborative expanded its vision to address teacher mentorship, induction, teacher effectiveness, and teacher preparation. This expansion can be traced to the annual Ford funding for CERI sites and an award from the Chicago Fund for Education Organizing, whose funds were matched one-on-one from the Communities for Public Education Reform. Collaborative members saw this progression in goals as vital and complementary to the GYO mission. The GYO consortium colleges were not always participants in discussions or activities surrounding these goals, and it is not known whether the new decisionmaking body involved them more deeply.

In the spring of 2009, the collaborative was attempting to advance these goals while making contingencies to address shortfalls should the legislature not pass continuing funds. It had grown to include seven organizations, and the executive directors from each organization were meeting every month. The GYO Partners Council had been formed to increase inclusiveness.

Urban Partnership Program and Former Collaborating for Education Reform Initiative 1 Sites

As a small part of this study, we surveyed former Ford Foundation sites from both the original UPPs (which ran from 1989 to 1991) and the CERI 1 sites (1998–2003). We insert this analysis here to provide further data on whether these types of collaboratives have been successful in sustaining themselves over time.

In 2002, we surveyed the 16 UPP sites. In 2009, we repeated the survey and included the CERI 1 sites as well. These telephone surveys were conducted with individuals who had leadership positions in the main organization involved in the initiative. The aim of the survey was to identify how many of the UPP and CERI 1 collaboratives continued to function and, if so, in what manner (e.g., the nature of the partnership, the mission, and funding sources).

The 2002 survey (N = 33 leaders surveyed) found that 12 of the 16 original UPP collaboratives were still functioning. All 12 collaboratives had the same mission; six had all the original partners; and all had additional partners. Respondents had remarkably similar views on what it took to sustain the collaborative, and these views are highly consistent with the larger literature (Hogue, 1994; Shirley, 1997; Warren, 2001): (1) a common vision that united the various partners; (2) nurturing of the partner relationships; (3) support from the highest levels of the partnering organizations; (4) committed, capable representatives with the authority to act on behalf of their organizations; (5) collaborative norms that all partners follow; (6) committed visionary leaders; and (7) sustained, stable funding sources.

Interviews with individuals from collaboratives that no longer existed confirmed these views. The reasons cited for no longer functioning included difficulty building relationships among partners and developing trust, inability to show impact, and no more funding.

In 2009, we attempted to track down the CERI 1 sites that did not continue into CERI 2 (five sites) and the remaining 12 UPP sites from 2002. Note that three of the UPP sites became CERI 1 sites, making a total of 14 collaboratives. We were able to track down 12: seven UPP/non–CERI 1 sites, three UPP/CERI 1 sites, and two former CERI 1 sites. However, after many attempts, we were able to interview individuals representing only seven collaboratives. Of these, only six were still functioning: three UPP only, two CERI 1 only (non-UPP), and one UPP/CERI 1 site. Of these six, only one reported maintaining all the original partners and also adding partners.

In sum, ten years after the end of the UPP initiative, one-third of the collaboratives had disappeared. Four UPP collaboratives (one-quarter of the total) still existed after 18 years. After six years, three of the five CERI 1 sites were functioning, and only one of these reported to be expanding.[2]

Summary of Progress Made, Enablers, and Constraints

In this section, we return to the question of whether the foundation's efforts helped produce functioning collaboratives that became independent of the foundation's funding. We found that AI in Austin appeared to be a well-functioning collaborative with significant interorganizational linkages and independent resources that was on a strong positive trajectory for growth. At the time of the last interviews, AI's efforts and political power at the local and state levels appeared to be consistently growing.

Chicago's GYO made important strides in setting up a collaborative to support specific legislation and to obtain funding for partners

---

[2]   We examined the literature to compare this survival rate with other collaborative efforts, but we could not identify any relevant studies or data.

to work together to implement the legislation. It consistently received state funding every year since FY 2006. The collaborative maintained strong connections, and partners worked together on pursuing mentoring and induction goals. It, however, had not yet established more-collaborative decisionmaking functions, especially with its consortium partners. Furthermore, much of the energy was focused on ensuring funding from the legislature (the general assembly) as educational services more generally were being cut. Therefore, although attempting to take on new directions, its growth seemed far more uncertain at that time.

In contrast to these two, the Alianza was functioning as part of a network of organizations interested in promoting reform in Puerto Rico, but with no common, central tenet for what reform to pursue or how it should be accomplished. AFM was in a state of stasis and uncertainty, due to an inability to secure alternative sources of funding for its collaborative process and a change in district administration. The relationship and collaborative processes developed were maintained throughout this period, and PPS and AFM Arts continued to work with the district offices that had been supportive in the past. DC VOICE met success in funding but functioned less as a collaborative and more as a single organization that partnered effectively with other organizations on specific issues of mutual benefit.

Looking across the CERI and UPP efforts as a whole, the evidence suggests that foundation funding was, in most cases, effective in supporting the creation of a collaborative. Without further foundation support, however, the future of several of the collaboratives was very uncertain. Our analysis across the case-study sites revealed several themes concerning barriers and enablers of collaborative function.

Collaborative Efforts Are Highly Susceptible to Constraints and Changes in the Environment

Beyond a shadow of a doubt, the environment in which the grantees operated affected whom they partnered with and their ability to become established and financially independent. The following examples illustrate the point.

Both Jackson and Puerto Rico were known from the outset for declining economies and weak philanthropic sectors. Thus, the ability of grantees in these locations to become self-sustaining would be highly dependent on securing funds from other foundations or the government sector. By the end of the initiative, the economic collapse suggested that these two sites in particular would have very difficult struggles for future financial support.

But besides the funding issue, the collaboratives had to establish working relationships with their respective school districts. In Puerto Rico, the district is the commonwealth Ministry of Education. Due to significant turnover in government parties and restructuring, the collaborative had difficulties finding constant partners with whom to work in the ministry. As key positions turned over and the ministry's priorities changed, the collaborative struggled to keep up.

Jackson experienced similar struggles, but for a shorter period of time. The collaborative flourished initially, with strong support in the initial years from the superintendent and her successor. During CERI 2, the superintendent faced a very public lawsuit, and the district underwent a very difficult budgetary period and slowed down reform efforts. In the final two years of the initiative, a new superintendent, a significantly new school board, and a new mayor came into office. Collectively, they held very different views of education from those of their predecessors and those held by the collaborative. While AFM valued collaborative processes to improve schools, the new administration favored central management. In addition, the mayor's arrest brought turmoil to the community and left the collaborative without strong supporters in the district or mayor's office. This community was ill prepared for a consensus response, the major recession hit, and funding dried up.

DC VOICE knew from its early efforts not to rely on high-level district leadership for sustained support—turnover was too rapid and predictable. It attempted to build relationships with midlevel members of the professional staff in the district office, but these positions proved to be just as fleeting. In 2007, the district and staffing were reorganized again when Mayor Adrian Fenty took over the city schools and Michele

Rhee became chancellor. Throughout this period, DC VOICE had to continually renew or create relationships.

The barriers to creating successful, functioning collaboratives in these environments are clear. What might be questioned is the theory of change—is it feasible to expect struggling CBOs to build collaboratives across equally struggling education organizations to support reform? Our case studies indicate that it is difficult for small, struggling collaboratives to succeed in sustaining education reform in an environment in which the large, existing education organizations themselves are unstable. Under these conditions, the collaboratives are more likely to expend their energies on continually recreating their relationships with the districts than to engage in efforts to improve education. The theory of change, especially when examining interorganizational linkages among small "players" within these large contexts, appears not to function as intended.

The Austin and Chicago grantees, which began with stronger economies and philanthropic sectors, were less embattled. Their superintendents, both recognized nationally for education reform, led the schools during CERI 2. In comparison with staff at the other sites, the midlevel staff remained generally stable, with little turnover in key positions.

In the examples above, Jackson and Puerto Rico economies continued to be unsupportive of nonprofit efforts, such as CERI 2, and turnover in district personnel hampered the collaboratives' efforts. A clear implication might be that encouraging the growth of collaboratives to fight the instability within the districts ignores the very real impact that district and economic instability will have on the fragile, newly forming collaboratives. Yet, AFM still maintained standing in the community and with district offices and was looked to for collaborative support, while the remnants of the Alianza located in Sacred Heart University sought new partners to promote that organization's vision of education in Puerto Rico.

Leadership Change Affected Collaborative Growth

In developing CERI, the foundation hoped that collaboratives would offer more leadership stability than districts had and act as a counterbalance to the purported revolving door at the top. Our findings indicate that grantees experienced leadership turnover and that leadership changes significantly affected the collaboratives' mission.

Earlier, we discussed the history of leadership within the Alianza and how it evolved from having very charismatic and well-known leaders to a series of successors with diminishing power due to falling revenues and lack of consensus among former members about a common mission. This is a clear example of how leadership matters over time.

However, some changes under new leaders brought about positive growth. In Austin, the new leader carefully reviewed what AI had accomplished up to that point. Under his leadership, AI returned to its church-based constituencies and took on new life by moving away from the focus on a pipeline and creating new partnerships with multiple organizations and affecting state and local education policies. Similarly, DC VOICE's change in leaders during CERI 2 brought in a person who built a strong board and secured further funding.

We conclude that leadership changes in the collaboratives were not uncommon and, as the literature review implied, were important to the trajectory of the collaborative work.

Inclusiveness in Leadership Plays an Important Role in Collaborative Building and Growth

The study confirms the overall picture painted from the literature review that collaborative leadership must be able to foster trusting relationships, effectively communicate the collaborative's goals and vision, involve collaborative members in decisionmaking, motivate them to act, and encourage reflection and improvement of strategies. We also found that collaboratives benefited when leaders reflected on the degree to which the collaborative's efforts were meeting the needs of their communities and identified whether changes in strategies were warranted.

AI's significant growth in collaboration best illustrates the importance of having a reflective, consensus-building leader. The change in leadership in 2007 brought about stronger participation of collaborative members for the pipeline initiative and a reevaluation of AI's former strategies. The new leader did not revive the Alliance cluster effort but identified a different and more-powerful strategy to promote teaching and learning. Under different leadership, AI collaborated with local and statewide organizations to build political clout and influence district and state educational policies. The new leader initiated more-collaborative data sharing, decisionmaking, and joint work. In contrast, collaborative leadership in Puerto Rico during CERI 2 lacked legitimacy and expertise for building collaboration and a common vision. This contributed to the collaborative's decline.

Building the Legitimacy of the Collaborative Proved Critical for Growth and Sustainment

The literature indicated that the legitimacy of leaders in the community could help propel collaboratives, but our work in CERI 1 indicated that, in the long term, collaboratives had to gain their own legitimacy as a "voice" for educational improvement. This analysis of CERI 2 showed that legitimacy was important in obtaining buy-in from key stakeholders, such as policymakers, district and school staff, community members, and parents. These constituencies faced competing demands for their time and were willing to cooperate with only those collaboratives that they perceived to be genuine and worthwhile. For example, in the case of AI, the collaborative did not make a convincing argument to the district as to why it needed to grant the Alliance schools more flexibility or autonomy. The district did not see the relevance of this particular activity to its local needs and was uncooperative.

Legitimacy also afforded collaboratives with the political clout and access needed to influence policymakers. Many different factors contributed to a collaborative's perceived legitimacy, including the reputation of the partner organizations, the perceived objectivity of the collaborative's approach, and the collaborative's ability to make a contribution to the solution of the problem at hand. For example, both AI and the GYO collaboratives consisted of CBOs that were connected and well respected within their communities and at the state level and had a history of working on educational issues. Their legitimacy strengthened the collaboratives' political reach and influence.

To cite a counterexample, during the last two years of CERI 2, DC VOICE placed more emphasis on community mobilizing than on cultivating partnerships with organizations that had established legitimacy in the policy arena. This weakened DC VOICE's influence because policymakers started viewing DC VOICE's research to be less objective than it had been in prior years.

Information Developing and Sharing and Joint Decisionmaking Supported Collaborative Function

The literature on successful collaboration describes common goals, joint work and decisionmaking, and shared information as essential to progress. In our sample, AI was a good example of a strong collaborative that grew significantly over time. The collaborative organizations worked very well as a team, and it was often difficult to trace attribution of an activity to one particular member. In the case of the teacher pipeline, much of the collaborative's work was jointly planned by AI, the colleges, and Capital IDEA. In its community-mobilizing work, AI worked very closely with community- and state-level organizations, shared information through forums, and involved different parties in decisionmaking through public stakeholder voting.

On the other hand, some CERI 2 sites fell short on information development, sharing, and joint decisionmaking. For example, in the case of Chicago's GYO, several college representatives stated that the CBOs did not share relevant information with them and excluded them from the decisionmaking process. This resulted in lack of coordination of pipeline activities across types of organizations. Although the CBOs had a common vision of systemic reform, this vision was not equally shared by the postsecondary institutions. The collaborative was attempting to remedy these issues in the spring of 2009.

Conflicts Among Partners Affected Some Efforts

The literature indicated that the road to collaboration is not without pitfalls. Conflict among partners is not unheard of and sometimes has deleterious effects. We saw such conflicts arise and note that to have been the case especially in the last two years of the effort, as tensions intensified across partner organizations as they struggled to sustain their own operations.

For example, it was clear by 2006 that the partners in the Alianza were beginning to go their separate ways to finding funding to support their specific organization's work. By 2006, the fee-for-service model was deemed inappropriate for the impoverished local districts, and the ministry was not following through with reform plans that would have strengthened the Alianza and strengthened its goals. The commonwealth budget crises prompted partners to look for resources to support their own missions. The Alianza, led by the university, provided fewer resources to the other partners, which, in turn, reduced their work under the Alianza.

Mission and funding conflicts also arose in Chicago, initially with conflict among organizations on the shape of the legislation. Although the foundation offered the services of LCN as a mediator to manage the conflict, the collaborative took a different path and excluded the organizations with competing views from any future participation in its efforts. Tensions also arose in later years when several universities that were local partners in consortia had their own teacher recruitment and development programs. Under the GYO teacher pipeline initiative, they provided professors at neighborhood sites and had to significantly underwrite their participation. Several indicated having second thoughts about their efforts with GYO because they felt that their own programs were less costly and more effective. Further, although the partners in the GYO collaborative appeared to work together well, it was clear from interviews that the local consortium partners did not always do so. We do not know whether later attempts to remedy this situation through the creation of a formal decisionmaking structure were effective.

Fundraising Needed to Be Attended to Early

We found that the grantees differed sharply in how they approached fundraising and building a diverse base of support. We did not find much evidence about fundraising in the literature, so we were uncertain whether the diversity found in this study is a common phenomenon within initiatives or not.

Two grantees, AI and GYO, made strategic decisions to seek funding for their efforts from sources other than foundations. As noted above, AI went back to its grassroots church members to create a sustainable pool of funding and political support that could be directed toward influencing state and local education policy. It also successfully advocated for more-stable funding support for specific pipeline partners, such as Capital IDEA, which provided wrap-around support for the teacher candidates.

Early on, Chicago's collaborative sought government support for the GYO pipeline and ensured this through government appropriations. Although this funding stream was under attack due to budget crises at the state level, over the first several years, it grew. And even for the future, the program is on the books as a state-supported program.

The new leader of DC VOICE began to immediately, more-seriously pursue new funding options and successfully brought in significant resources from multiple foundations.

The point here is that these grantees were very deliberate in their decisions to seek multiple sources of funding, rather than rely on the same foundations. They called together collaborative members to ensure that their approach could be carried out, and future funding was not put off as a concern but tackled early on.

The Alianza and AFM sought grant funding from foundations, with some early success. However, they did not successfully expand their funding base before the end of the CERI grant. Once the recession hit and affected foundation giving, they were left with few options.

CHAPTER FOUR

Progress Toward Goals

The organizations at each site were not just supposed to form collaboratives. The collaboratives had to engage in activities that would ultimately lead to improved outcomes for students. In this chapter, we analyze the progress made toward the three activity goals the foundation set: development and implementation of activities to support quality in teaching and learning; development and implementation of activities to promote system-wide policy changes; and development as a "voice" for a broad group of stakeholders. We divide the discussion into four parts to address research questions 1b, 1c, and 2 as they relate to collaborative activities. First, we document the major activities undertaken by the grantees. We then discuss whether the choices were reasonable. Third, we look in detail at the activities undertaken by the individual sites and assess their implementation progress. Finally, we draw out themes across the sites to describe what factors enabled or constrained their progress.

Summary of Activities Undertaken

A major decision that the grantees had to make under the CERI effort was how to focus their energies to bring about sustained improvements in their local districts. The foundation did not dictate a set of specific activities for grantees to pursue; it only encouraged them to address the goals. More particularly, the foundation has had a long history of promoting grantee independence in this area and in encouraging its grantees to develop ideas most suitable to the local context.

In contrast to how it handled CERI 1, the foundation did not provide technical assistance to CERI 2 grantees to think through their strengths and weaknesses and develop appropriate interventions. While the three CERI 1 grantees had at least some support under the original initiative (through the LCN), new CERI 2 grantees were left to their own devices.

Table 4.1 outlines the major activities proposed by the grantees under the three activity goals that Ford established. Because local conditions and priorities are subject to change, some grantees added new activities over time. Activities that were adopted after the start of CERI 2 are marked in gray.

Several observations can be made. First, the type of activities and the ways in which they were expected to promote teaching and learning varied dramatically across the sites. Some sites chose activities or interventions that were designed to affect teaching and learning directly. For example, the Alianza and AFM focused on providing professional development and leadership training to districts or groups of schools within districts. Other grantees, such as AI, GYO, and DC VOICE, chose policy interventions. AI and GYO decided to implement teacher pipelines to address the issue of teacher quality in hard-to-staff schools in their communities. DC VOICE focused on advocating for improved teaching and learning by conducting its own research and disseminating the results to parents and the wider community.

Second, some grantees shifted their focus or added new activities over the years as a result of changes in external or internal conditions. For example, changes in AI's leadership brought issues of student assessment and accountability systems to the forefront. In the case of DC VOICE, changes in the structure of the district central office led DC VOICE to restrategize and adopt new activities, such as action-based research and community mobilizing.

Third, in several instances, grantees did not propose specific activities for each of the three categories. Specifically, "becoming a voice" for the community was originally not in the proposals; however, several grantees joined into a process resembling this fairly early. For example, DC VOICE originally proposed gathering research and applying it to the D.C. context, then putting out newsletters that include objec-

Table 4.1
Proposed Activities to Address Collaborating for Education Reform Initiative 2 Goals

Indicators	The Alianza	AFM	AI	DC VOICE	GYO
Promote quality in teaching and learning	Provide fee-for-service support to districts	Provide professional development, counselor training, college activities	Establish a mini-district	N/A	N/A
Promote policies that lead to quality teaching and learning	Establish a parent office in ministry; create a research institute	Scale Lanier innovations to district and state (e.g., college day, college planning tool, new standards)	Develop teacher pipeline pathways and articulations; Change state policy on testing time and testing regime; create more future standards	Advocate for policies that support SQT; produce Ready Schools and other reports; Action research	Ensure that the state passes GYO law; promote funding and improvement to GYO law; implement consortium approach to state's teacher pipeline program
Become a voice for the underserved population and sustained reform	N/A	Become voice in community for collaborative approaches	Become voice for state reforms; Mobilize church members to work with high-poverty, low-performing schools	Become voice for research-based reforms with participation by underserved communities; monitor changes that support SQT	N/A

NOTE: N/A = not applicable; the indicator was not part of the original proposal, and no activities were later undertaken.

tive research data and findings to the community to create a more-informed populace in a sometimes highly polarized and cacophonous debate. Later in the initiative, this was recognized as creating a voice in the community. In Austin, AI began community organizing around the negative impacts of the testing regime adopted by the state several years into the initiative and began to call this set of activities acting as the voice of the community.

Were Choices Reasonable?

As discussed in Chapter Two, this study did not set out to assess the impact that grantees' activities would have on student performance. Nonetheless, it is possible to broadly assess whether their choices were reasonable mechanisms for improvement. We developed several criteria for judging "reasonableness" within the CERI context.

An activity might be deemed reasonable if (1) the activity appeared central to improving student outcomes and not otherwise provided within the district or by other organizations; (2) a prima facie case could be made that it might positively affect student achievement over the period of the grant; (3) it could be supported by some research base showing positive effects on student outcomes or schooling more generally; (4) it could reasonably be accomplished in that it would not require significant supplemental resources unavailable to the district or CBOs when taken to scale; and (5) it would be within the expected powers of the collaborative to implement within the five-year duration of the grant.

Table 4.2 shows our assessment of the reasonableness of the major choices made according to the above five criteria. The table cells are colored green if the grantees' ideas seemed to have merit according to the specific criteria above. The cell is marked yellow if there was some merit, based on specific assumptions. For example, implementing parental involvement programs in schools has been shown to have impact, but only if the program is a high-quality one with specifically measurable goals. Thus, the impact is dependent on the grantee iden-

Table 4.2
Reasonableness of Goals and Activities

Major Activity	Needed in Community and Not Otherwise Provided	Prima Facie Case for Five-Year Impact	Research Base or Prior Implementation	Scalable with Normal Resources	Implementable by Partners
Create teacher pipelines (AI, GYO)	Both districts had hard-to-staff schools. Both districts had several programs intended to address this issue.	The optimistic length of time before the first cohort graduated was more than six years.	There was virtually no research support for this type of effort. What was available showed very low rates of completion.	Both sites chose models requiring significant wrap-around services and, in certain cases, expensive four-year schools. Low rates of completion would drive per-teacher costs up.	Sites did not always partner with optimal colleges to implement the programs.
Create a mini-district (AI)	There was no established need other than specific groups' dissatisfaction with the implementation of state standards and testing regimes.	No case was made.	There was no research base. There were no prior cases of a CBO managing a mini-district.	No work specified the added cost, but the additional administrative layer would likely add to the resource burden.	AI and other organizations had no prior experience with running a district. It would have to gain state exemption to implement.

Table 4.2—Continued

Major Activity	Needed in Community and Not Otherwise Provided	Prima Facie Case for Five-Year Impact	Research Base or Prior Implementation	Scalable with Normal Resources	Implementable by Partners
Mobilize the community to demand reforms (AI, DC VOICE)	Low community involvement in schools was noted at each site. The district was seen as a fortress.	The grantees can make a basic case assuming that the focus is on interventions that have impact. They can make a long-range case for greater general support of public education.	There is little education research base. Programs are rooted primarily in a political theory argument.	Activities are scalable if the grantee can get funding beyond the Ford grant.	AI had expertise in this area. DC VOICE had limited experience.
Provide professional development and other development services (AFM, Alianza)	Human resource capacity is recognized as low. The Alianza and AFM communities had low funding levels for professional development.	Grantees can make a basic case, assuming that there is high-quality professional development targeting teacher, principal, and counselor needs.	There is weak correlation between professional development and student improvement. The effect depends on the quality of the services.	Programs could be sustained with a reasonable amount of funds, if districts had funds to support a scale-up.	Both grantees had established records of strong service provision.

Table 4.2—Continued

Major Activity	Needed in Community and Not Otherwise Provided	Prima Facie Case for Five-Year Impact	Research Base or Prior Implementation	Scalable with Normal Resources	Implementable by Partners
Increase parental involvement (AFM, Alianza, AI)	All the communities needed improved parental involvement. AFM, AI, and the Alianza had few existing programs to address this.	Grantees can make a basic case that high-quality programs could have an impact. The effect would depend on the specific focus.	There is weak correlation between parental involvement and student improvement. The effect depends on the quality of the program.	Programs could be sustained through minimum funds, if districts had funds to support a scale-up.	Grantees have expertise in this area.
Create a research institute (Alianza)	There is no such entity in Puerto Rico.	Grantees could make the basic case that one could be formed and functioning in the time period but not how it would affect student achievement.	There is no specific research on this. What research there is is based on prior lab-school histories.	The institute could be sustained with a PRCF-provided grant.	Grantees had the needed expertise.

Table 4.2—Continued

Major Activity	Needed in Community and Not Otherwise Provided	Prima Facie Case for Five-Year Impact	Research Base or Prior Implementation	Scalable with Normal Resources	Implementable by Partners
Conduct research and disseminate results on issues that support quality of teaching (DC VOICE)	There is a lack of organizations in the community holding DCPS accountable. There is a lack of knowledge and transparency in the community pertaining to DCPS and its policies on QTL.	Grantees can make a case assuming that research focuses on issues that directly affect student learning and outcomes. They can make a long-range case for greater general support of public education.	There is no specific research on this; the effect depends on issues addressed by research, types of changes adopted, and how they are implemented.	Activities could be sustained if the grantee can get funding beyond the Ford grant.	Grantees have experience in this area.

NOTE: Red means that the idea largely did not meet the criteria for reasonableness. Yellow means that the idea meets some of the criteria. Green means that the idea meets most of the criteria. QTL = quality of teaching and learning.

tifying and putting in place a well-thought-out program keyed to specific goals. The cell is marked red if the idea fails to meet the criteria.

The assessments were made in the following manner. First, we reviewed the literature, relying heavily on recent summative reviews, to determine whether it had a strong research base. In reviewing the literature, we did not attempt to evaluate the research designs (i.e., give more weight to randomized controlled trials than to correlational analyses), but to assess what the body of research suggested for a particular intervention. In many cases, we could not identify any literature to suggest that the intervention had been undertaken before and had strong positive effects. We interviewed district staff to understand whether the district had need for such programs or interventions. We interviewed the collaborative partners to determine whether the partners had done something similar before and whether they had the capacity or could acquire the capacity to do so again. Primarily through interviews and a review of the costs of the interventions when known, we determined whether the implemented program could be scaled up and sustained with available funds. By drawing on different sources of evidence, we could develop an overall picture of "reasonableness."

The main finding from this analysis is that the grantees did not always make reasonable choices as assessed by these criteria. Although, in many instances, the grantees appropriately identified the needs in their communities and had the appropriate collaborative partners, they did not consistently make reasonable choices in the activities adopted to address these needs. First, most sites did not invoke either prima facie or research evidence to justify or argue for their chosen interventions.

For example, AI and GYO selected the development and implementation of teacher pipelines not only to ameliorate teacher shortages and high turnover rates in their communities but also to provide jobs for the underemployed as a means to spark community development. Their initiatives targeted teachers' aides or parent leaders in the communities to become teachers, many of whom would need a full four years of college to meet graduation requirements. The sites justified the pipeline as the means for ensuring jobs for the unemployed and underemployed by making teachers of adults who could "understand their children." These sites did not consider alternative designs that might have maximized recruiting more–academically skilled candidates or those needing fewer college credits to qualify. Several representatives argued that the initiative should not be judged by how it affected students but by how it affected employment and individual efficacy of the adults. Furthermore, we found little research to support such an intervention, and none linking these types of interventions to student outcomes. One GYO partner had developed a similar pipeline, supported by a large U.S. Department of Education grant prior to CERI 2, but its final outcomes had not been evaluated. The program had not graduated or placed teachers and was struggling to provide the supports needed given the length of time participants were taking to graduate. Thus, their decision to support a pipeline in CERI 2 appeared to be based as much on economic mission concerns as on education concerns. As one respondent wrote, the decision was based on the collaborative members' "knowledge of their local school and which parents and paraprofessionals would make strong teachers, based on their multiple assets and their strong ties to the community and to the students."

Similarly, AI's plan to create a semiautonomous mini-district was based more on political arguments than concrete thinking concerning its organizational capacity or likely impacts on children. The grantee was frustrated, perhaps justly, over what it saw as the tendency of the district to overtest children in a high-stakes testing regime and simultaneously reduce the time for nontested subjects in the school. Proponents saw increased decisionmaking power over a group of schools as a way to establish the content and pedagogy they desired. But the group had little curricular expertise and only vague governance plans.

In contrast, interventions pertaining to professional development and parent training, provided that they are well designed, have been documented in the literature as being positively correlated with student performance. The sites could make a prima facie case that these types of interventions might help propel quality teaching and learning. Thus, activities led by AFM and parent training led by AI made sense so long as they were not duplicative of the districts' activities.

Second, the grantees did not always think through the implementation assumptions they were making, create plans to address them, or identify ways to sustain them. For example, the Alianza's proposed set of professional development services was based on a fee-for-service model in a commonwealth economy in decline. Public funding of all programs was in jeopardy. In addition, the professional development services provided focused on individualization and project-based, in-depth learning just as the country began to move toward greater accountability using high-stakes testing—the antithesis of the Alianza approach. Finally, in the prior five years, the group had not fully substantiated claims that its model could have strong positive effects on test scores. Thus, it appeared unrealistic to expect schools to pay for such professional development in the absence of firm proof of its efficacy.

This is not to say that professional development was not needed, perhaps in each district. The provision of otherwise-unavailable professional development in Puerto Rico and Jackson made sense if the collaboratives made appropriate choices about what to provide and could implement those choices in an effective, sustainable manner. Activities to encourage parental involvement also made sense, assuming that they were of high quality, not otherwise provided, and sustainable. It was incumbent on the emerging collaborative to ensure that these conditions would be met during implementation.

Summary of Progress Toward Goals

We analyzed progress toward the stated goals of each collaborative under the three areas indicated in prior chapters: promote quality in teaching and learning, promote policies that lead to quality in teaching and learning, and become a voice for the underrepresented and for sustained reform. We reviewed the interview notes from previous years, as well as the original MOUs before the final interview with the study sites. During the final interviews, we specifically asked about each set of activities they had undertaken.

Table 4.3 shows that the sites varied widely in their implementation of proposed activities. For example, the Alianza accomplished few of the goals it proposed in CERI 2, while GYO created the pipeline it set out to establish. Table 4.3 reports the indicators presented in Table 4.1, with color-coding indicating the level of implementation. In

Table 4.3
Level of Implementation of Activities by Sites

Indicators	Alianza	AFM	AI	DC VOICE	GYO
Promote quality in teaching and learning	Provide fee-for-service support to districts	Provide professional development, counselor training, college activities	Establish a mini-district	N/A	N/A
Promote policies that lead to quality in teaching and learning	Establish a parent office in ministry	Scale Lanier innovations to district and state (e.g., college day, college planning tool, new standards)	Develop teacher pipeline pathways and articulations; change state policy on testing time and testing regime	Advocate for policies that support SQT; produce Ready Schools and other reports	Ensure that the state passes GYO law; promote funding and improvement to GYO law; implement consortium approach to state's teacher pipeline program
	Create a research institute		Create more future standards		
Become a voice for underserved population and sustained reform	N/A	Become a voice in the community for collaborative approaches	Become a voice for state reforms; mobilize church members to work with high-poverty, low-performing schools	Become voice for research-based reforms with participation by underserved communities; monitor changes that support SQT	N/A

NOTE: N/A = not applicable; the indicator was not part of the original proposal. Red means that the goal was largely not accomplished or was still in the planning stages. Yellow means that the goal was partially accomplished. Green means that the goal was largely accomplished.

the table, red shading indicates those goals that were not accomplished or that, at best, remained in the planning phase. Yellow indicates goals that were partially accomplished, and green indicates goals that were essentially accomplished.

As can be seen, the grantees found mixed success implementing quality in teaching and learning programs. AFM successfully promoted teaching and learning through professional development. However, efforts to provide fee-for-service professional development (the Alianza) or autonomous mini-districts (AI) were not fully implemented or sustained.

Grantees successfully promoted policy changes to support quality in teaching and learning. For example, GYO fought for and established legislation supporting a teacher pipeline—a major accomplishment. Both AI and GYO established relationships among providers to support teacher pipelines, ensured the development of articulation agreements across an array of higher-education institutions that had not existed before, developed the student support services needed, and ensured that higher-education institutions developed the career pathways needed. The pipelines, however, suffered dropout and replacement problems and required continuing wrap-around services. The universities and districts have other programs in place that appear to be effective in placing qualified teachers into hard-to-staff schools. The Alianza promoted a parent office in the Ministry of Education, and this was adopted as policy. AFM scaled up several interventions developed in the Lanier feeder pattern to have them adopted more widely by the district or state. DC VOICE launched a series of action-based research efforts and disseminated its findings to promote better supports for quality in teaching.

Finally, at the end of the effort, two of the grantees (AI and DC VOICE) began to focus strongly on becoming a voice for the underserved in the community and developing community leaders, while, for the other collaboratives, this was less of a focus.

In the next sections, we describe each site's activities and progress in more detail.

The Alianza

At the beginning of CERI 2, the Alianza had completed the development of a collaborative process for schools that promoted fact-finding and group reflection processes as the means to review their performance and develop stronger plans for improvement. The systemic change process included support for staff to create a unifying vision for educational excellence and the means to meet those visions, visits to high-performing schools to observe how their classrooms worked to serve all students, adoption of progressive pedagogical practices, improvements to student counseling by use of specific instruments developed in CERI 1, the development of teacher and parent leaders, and the adoption of a specific course in the middle grades devoted to youth development and critical thinking. The Alianza was working in five districts to implement these actions, and facilitators in each district supported the connections between the Alianza and the district activities. The Ford Foundation funding was used to support professional development and materials, as well as the facilitators.

In addition, the Secretary of Education had selected the Alianza's program as one of five promising interventions that other districts could adopt, noting that it was the best for systemic change approaches. It hoped to start a major initiative to blend the lessons learned across the five successful interventions to improve education in the commonwealth.

The original plan for CERI 2 was to simultaneously spread the intervention to more districts and enhance its implementation in the five early adopters. As discussed in Chapter Three, it called for the creation of an education policy institute (IPEDCo) to further promote, develop, and demonstrate promising practices in Puerto Rico.

These plans were never achieved. First, budget issues meant that the commonwealth and the Ministry of Education were hard pressed to keep schools open, much less promote improvements. Second, the Alianza proved unable to gain further funding for its efforts through the ministry or through local or national foundations. Finally, leaders within the Alianza moved on to other positions in CBOs or the ministry leaving the collaborative in less-experienced hands during a period of significant institutional challenge. Over the course of the five years, the Alianza's joint activities slowly dissolved.

We note that the Alianza had never stated any goal concerning becoming a voice for the underserved or underrepresented, so we do not address this area in our analysis.

Promote Quality in Teaching and Learning

The Alianza proposed a fee-for-service model to support the district activities to improve teaching and learning, but districts proved unable to support such fees. By 2007, when the Alianza could no longer support the work of the facilitators, it reported difficulty in maintaining relationships with any of the districts. Selected activities from the portfolio continued in a few schools, but usually without the professional development or personnel previously provided by the collaborative. The schools and districts reported keeping some process improvements, such as working across districts to lobby the Ministry of Education for support and writing proposals to gain grants. However, in the absence of the facilitator position and the Alianza funding and technical support, in 2008, district personnel reported that the majority of interventions had vanished. While the initial activities undertaken with the five districts might have affected students, the data gathered by the Alianza showed very inconsistent results. Data collected in Puerto Rico were insufficient to reliably assess impact.

The Ministry of Education's promotion of five existing educational initiatives in Puerto Rico, including IPEDCo, appeared to have foundered, with reportedly no actions taking place to promote these ideas from 2007 onward.

Promote Policies That Lead to Quality in Teaching and Learning

By 2007, the Alianza had transformed into IPEDCo, a policy institute designed to affect education policy in Puerto Rico. IPEDCo tried to raise awareness about its mission by holding public policy forums with the community. However, interviewees reported that the policy forums did not reach a widening circle of people. Initially, the Alianza/IPEDCo taped and aired broadcasts about major educational issues and specific improvements being made in schools across Puerto Rico.

By 2008, it had discontinued filming new television broadcasts and ran old episodes out of Sacred Heart University trying to associate positive change in the educational system with the activities of the institute. Our last interviews indicated that the institute had not yet produced documents or products that noticeably affected policy. Its major project—to understand the importance of the functions of a school district system—was intended to place the institute in a position to make recommendations to the Ministry of Education on needed changes in the school district structure. Furthermore, a study on other education legislation, designed to put IPEDCo in a position to make policy recommendations in the future, had not made any clear progress, and no specific publication plans were evident.

An exception is that, in 2006, the Ministry of Education recognized the importance of parents in students' success. A policy statement was issued requiring every district in Puerto Rico to incorporate parent participation in the district-level decisionmaking. The policy statement was written in coordination with a panel of parents, which included Alianza parent leaders. In 2007, the permanent office for parents in the Ministry of Education was established and was active throughout the island at the time of our 2008 visit. It remains to be seen whether the new administration will continue to support this office.

Ask for More

In 2004, JPS, in general, had been experiencing difficulty in meeting the goals of No Child Left Behind (Pub. L. 107-110). At the time the CERI study was initiated, the Lanier cluster schools had the lowest performance scores in the district. Thus, the collaborative focused on providing direct services to the Lanier cluster schools in four main areas: professional development, college and career access, school climate and communication, and parent leadership. The purposes of these interventions were to promote quality in teaching and learning through developing teacher skills and principal leadership, and to increase student interest in going to college and parents' involvement in their children's schooling. AFM had not articulated a purpose of becoming a voice in the community for the underrepresented or underserved, but it did articulate a goal of becoming a voice for collaborative approaches.

Promote Quality in Teaching and Learning

The collaborative developed activities in several areas to promote quality in teaching and learning.

Principal Collaboration and Professional Development. As part of CERI 1, AFM supported the development of a principal's academy, which provided a forum for Lanier pattern principals to work together on feeder-pattern issues, such as better transitions between grade levels, poor performance in specific areas across the grade levels, and better sharing of information on individual students across grade levels to ensure that they were placed properly and received needed services. It continued into CERI 2 with the principals meeting on a regular basis to discuss common issues, plan solutions, undertake visits and walk-throughs of each other's schools, and conduct similar activities. AFM provided significant professional development as requested by the principals and encouraged sharing of ideas across the grade levels, visiting each others' schools and using existing protocols for assessing the strengths and weaknesses of each school. These activities were maintained throughout CERI 2. In 2007, JPS developed a leadership institute to train personnel to become principals. This incorporated some of the best practices and ideas from the AFM initiative but was no longer run by AFM. It represents an institutionalization of the AFM activities.

AFM's work in this area led to increased and systematic meetings among the principals, who continued to meet once a month to address the needs of their schools, to discuss district-wide issues, and to ensure that their work complemented each others' and the district's initiatives. Two senior principals in the Lanier cluster also acted as coaches for the more-junior principals to increase collaboration. Furthermore, AFM hired a retired superintendent to mentor the new principals and to support principal coaches at the Lanier schools by providing advice and guidance and by conducting learning walks to assess school needs.

Professional Development for Teachers. AFM also provided professional development opportunities for Lanier-feeder-pattern teachers up until 2008. Teacher trainings often took place on Saturdays, with AFM picking up the cost of teacher stipends for the extra day. Typically, five sessions (four hours per session) of training were provided annually. At times, these trainings involved all Lanier cluster teachers of particular grade levels or subject areas. In other instances, lead teachers received the training and were tasked with sharing it with other teachers in their school.

Each year, the training sessions had a different emphasis, determined by AFM and the Lanier school principals. The topics addressed included math and reading instructional pedagogy, data use for decisionmaking, state curriculum requirements, and curriculum alignment across elementary, middle, and high school levels within the feeder pattern. The cross-level collaboration of teachers encouraged by the trainings led to the identification of discontinuities in the state standards for mathematics, which AFM brought to the attention of the state.

The intensity of the teacher professional development diminished or decreased significantly over time. By 2009, AFM stopped providing teacher professional development for several reasons. First, AFM was running out of funds and had to make a decision regarding which services to terminate. AFM selected teacher professional development because it was more costly than other AFM interventions. Second, the Mississippi standards, curriculum, and assessments had placed new demands and pressures on JPS and its schools, including the Lanier schools. Teachers had little time to participate in AFM professional development or experiment with new classroom strategies advocated by AFM. Third, the district started literacy-teacher professional development as a result of the new state curriculum and assessment, making AFM's professional development less essential.

An anticipated outcome of teacher professional development was for Lanier cluster teachers to develop a literacy-articulation rubric. The rubric was completed in fall 2009, with training taking place for one literacy coach in each school in the feeder pattern during 2009. The rubric represented a vertical alignment of curriculum, fifth grade through twelfth grade. It aimed to help teachers identify knowledge, skill, and content areas that needed to be covered at each grade level and to use similar terminologies to help ease transitions for their students between grades and school levels. AFM representatives hoped to have the rubric adopted by the district. They report, however, that it was neither fully implemented in the Lanier cluster schools nor adopted by JPS.

Promote Access to and Interest in College. To increase student interest and access to college, AFM implemented several activities. The Lanier cluster conducted College Spirit Day in 2002–2003 and continued that activity annually through our last site visit in 2009. At College Spirit Day, high-level college representatives visited schools and met with students to provide them with college-going counseling. This program was adopted by the district and was being held annually across the district with a permanent date on the district calendar. In addition, it began a Financial Aid Night, on which parents with their potential college-going children could meet with counselors to help them access and fill out the federal financial aid forms and other avenues of financial assistance.

AFM also developed a college checklist and wrote a brochure about what children needed to know to succeed at various stages of school. Lanier counselors also met together on a monthly basis to develop a counseling guide and forms (e.g., cards filled out by students that noted their preferences for courses for the next years, called *choice cards*) that helped ensure uniformity and coordination of courses across grade levels. The guide also helped identify students in need of assistance.

School Climate and Communication. AFM also focused on improving the school climate through the development of a rubric of processes and standards to improve the culture and operation of the schools in the feeder pattern. Although the principals of the Lanier cluster completed the development of the rubric, they reported that it was only partially implemented in three of the ten cluster schools. Those three schools were using the rubric during the learning walks to rate various aspects of their schools (e.g., safety, cleanliness, student engagement). Principals in the remaining schools were unfamiliar with the school-culture rubric and did not have plans to adopt it.

Parent Leadership Institute. AFM also implemented the Parent Leadership Institute (PLI) starting in 2006 and trained 30 parents each year thereafter, with approximately one-third of those coming from Lanier cluster schools. PPS, the CBO that was the fiduciary agent for AFM, experienced some difficulties in recruiting Lanier cluster parents and, in 2007–2008, expanded the recruitment pool to include JPS alumni who expressed an interest in "giving back" to the district. During the institute program, parents reviewed legislation and heard presentations from district and school representatives about issues that JPS faced and expectations for parent involvement. Parents were also trained on how to use data and read test results. Some of the parents went back to their schools and started their own projects, such as a father mentoring program and a mother-daughter book club. Other parents took a more-supportive role, such as working in the parent resource center at their children's school. The extent of parental involvement depended on parents' motivation and their schools' expectations. Many of the projects or activities implemented by PLI parents were limited in scope and likely had limited impact on student performance.

Promote Policies That Lead to Quality in Teaching and Learning

AFM's goal was to develop interventions in the Lanier feeder pattern and bring them to scale in the district and perhaps the state. Its efforts resulted in the district and state adopting several interventions, such as the following:

- The district adopted AFM's model of principal collaboration and mentorship. The district encouraged principals within feeder patterns to meet on a regular basis, and the district assigned additional mentors to ensure that all principals in all schools received one-on-one mentoring.
- In 2007, JPS established its own Principal Leadership Institute, which provided training for principals throughout the district.
- The discontinuities in the state standards for math that were indentified through AFM activities were remedied by the state with improved standards.
- Both College Spirit Day and Financial Aid Night were adopted by the district. The district also adopted the college checklist

and college brochure. These have since been adopted by the state department of education.

- The choice cards and transition forms were adopted by the district and used by all counselors. The counselor guide was completed in 2008 and was being piloted in the feeder pattern in 2008–2009. If the pilot is deemed to have gone well, AFM hopes that the district will adopt the counselor guide.

Become a Voice for Collaboration

Throughout both CERI 1 and CERI 2, AFM did not declare a goal of becoming a voice within the community for the underserved or underrepresented. By its last several years, as described in the previous chapter, it had become a voice for collaborative approaches to reform, and others in the community looked to AFM to promote collaborative efforts at reform. Thus, in discussions with the new superintendent and board, it advocated for partnership with other organizations, as well as the continuation of activities, such as the principal's academy and other forms of cross-site sharing. These approaches were favored by those who had been promoted from Lanier into the district central offices. However, with the significant changes in administration that began to strongly favor top-down management strategies, AFM struggled to maintain this voice in the community.

Austin Interfaith

AI implemented several activities aimed at promoting teaching and learning. Some of the activities were designed to influence policies at the district and state levels, while others were interventions provided directly to schools.

Promote Quality in Teaching and Learning

AI established a mini-district in order to continue organizing and expanding the Alliance Initiative schools under a feeder pattern. The goal was to create a cluster of AISD schools with alternative assessments, increased parental involvement, and a greater sense of autonomy and flexibility within schools to improve teaching and learning.

AI's effort to create the Alliance cluster of schools was not successful. AISD did not grant flexibility to Alliance schools. Some interviewees indicated that part of the explanation for this fallout was the fact that AI's activities coincided with competing district efforts. First, AI's effort was undertaken at the same time as AISD attempted to exert more control over schools (following concerns over test scores and accountability requirements). Others noted that AI's move to establish Alliance cluster schools occurred at the time AISD realigned the area superintendents to oversee grade levels. The district was already implementing its own concept of cluster schools, in which schools having a common area of interest worked together through committees comprised of principals, teachers, and district advisers. According to the central office staff, this structure moved schools away from top-down governance and gave them a stronger decisionmaking role. The two approaches were in conflict: The Alliance favored geographical clustering in a feeder pattern, while the district model favored clustering based on shared areas of interest.

Promote Policies That Lead to Quality in Teaching and Learning

AI attempted to influence policy in several ways, including the development of arrangements among institutional partners for a teacher pipeline, changes to state policy, and the creation of future standards.

Teacher Pipeline. One of the major activities undertaken by the Austin collaborative was the development of an alternative teacher pipeline. Its activities in this area resulted in articulation agreements among the college and university partners and furthered their interest in creating easier articulation across more career pathways.

The goal was to ameliorate teacher shortages experienced by AISD schools in the areas of bilingual education, special education, and math and science. AI and other organizations did not report to us any specific research they used to design the pipeline, but they heavily emphasized its connection to their mission and the similarity with its existing sets of services provided by Capital IDEA—a CBO developed by AI to help community members complete two-year technical degrees by offering wrap-around services and other supports. Because the former AI leadership who started the collaborative had a job development mission, the teacher pipeline was designed to train low-income paraprofessionals to enable them to become certified teachers to fill teaching-position vacancies and simultaneously improve their wages.

AI collaborated with a community college, private four-year colleges, and Capital IDEA—organizations with expertise in the development and implementation of such programs. However, not all the partners had sufficient resources to ensure adequate financial support to the teacher candidates. The collaborative's choice of private, four-year colleges over public colleges for the delivery of teacher-education courses meant higher student tuition. The collaborative had to continually struggle to obtain financial support to reduce tuition costs so that the teacher candidates would be able to continue along the pipeline. Partnering with the community college and Capital IDEA, on the other hand, helped reduce the financial burden on candidates, but only for costs associated with developmental class tuition and the wrap-around services. As indicated in Chapter Three, Capital IDEA is a job training corporation that is supported by county, state, and federal grants. Capital IDEA was able to use a portion of its funds to provide counseling to all pipeline teacher candidates, as well as to provide books, transportation, day care, and tuition reduction to candidates whose income fell to 200 percent below the poverty line.

However, because the teacher candidates had full-time jobs and sometimes lacked the appropriate academic preparation, they took longer to graduate than the candidates in traditional teacher-education programs and had low retention in the program. Of the 32 teacher candidates recruited (13 in bilingual-education cohort 1; 15 in the special-education cohort; and three in the math cohort), nine dropped out (four from bilingual education and five from special education). By 2009, none of the 32 candidates whom AI had recruited had graduated. With an estimated average of six years to complete the program, it was expensive for Capital IDEA to maintain the wrap-around services. According to some interviewees, Capital IDEA's training programs in other fields (e.g., health and technical fields) took less time to complete, were less expensive, and had better returns in terms of salaries. Even if all the remaining candidates graduate, the number of graduates will not meet the needs of AISD. At best, the teacher pipeline provided an additional marginal, and relatively expensive, source for teachers, beyond the established, university-based teacher-preparation programs.

Although this particular pathway faces challenges, the organizations involved emphasize that the collaborative put in place articulation agreements among several different local institutions and helped to clarify the career pathways within and across those institutions. Furthermore, these same institutions have gone on, based on their successful efforts here, to establish further articulation agreements and develop more career pathways between the two-year and four-year colleges. They see this effort as part of the legacy of the collaborative.

Parent Training to Promote Advocacy. AI has a history of teaching parents to become leaders in the community. Although the district provided general training for all its parent support specialists, AI provided additional training and retreats for those assigned to the Alliance schools in the district. During those sessions, parent support specialists were exposed to current issues that schools faced, including testing and accountability, and were trained to converse more effectively with parents, identify leaders, run a meeting, and involve and organize parents in schools. According to AI interviews and principals, parent support specialists in Alliance schools played leadership roles, while those in other district schools were more likely to take on administrative tasks, such as connecting parents to the appropriate service providers. In 2007, AISD hired a former AI member and an Alliance school principal to lead the district's parent initiative and training of parent support specialists. This resulted in modest changes in the district's training program to include a leadership component.

Community Mobilizing and the Development of Alternative Assessments. AI's unsuccessful efforts in establishing a mini-district led the organization to reevaluate its strategy for improving schools. AI recognized that, in order to improve schools, it needed to address policies at both the local and state levels. AI's interest was in policies related to current student assessment and accountability systems, as these systems had diminished school autonomy by placing new pressures and demands on schools. AI's activities involved building institutional capacity and mobilizing community and religious congregations, businesses (e.g., chamber of commerce), teacher unions, and sister organizations to put pressure on policymakers at the local and state levels. AI worked jointly with Education Austin (teachers' association) and other organizations to change AISD and state policies to incorporate a broader range of education assessments and propose a modified state accountability system. Together, they advocated for a bill on accountability. Although the bill did not pass, the legislative session did pass a revised version that prohibited schools from spending more than 10 percent of instructional time teaching to the state test. The legislative session also set up a governor's select committee on testing accountability, thus enabling AI to review and study issues regarding state accountability and to testify at hearings across the state. AI and Education Austin leaders testified publicly before the governor's select committee on several occasions regarding the testing regime in Texas. As a result, new legislation was introduced that called for (1) multiple student assessments and (2) moving away from sanctioning schools based on an adequate-yearly-progress growth model. AI also engaged the chamber of commerce (which is influential with the school board) in its effort to develop a new assessment system. Together, to inform the design of the new assessments, AI and the chamber were identifying the type of knowledge and skills the Austin economy would need. New approaches to assessment were expected by 2009 but were not developed at the time of our visit.

AI also conducted more than 50 research actions with businesses and educational leaders to discuss needs and brainstormed with community and education organization members. AI leaders conducted hundreds of house meetings with congregation members, organized accountability sessions, and convened an education summit to discuss various educational issues, mobilize the public, and ask for public commitment and funding.

Last, AI used its mobilization strategy to involve congregations in improving underperforming elementary schools in Austin's south side. This approach was different from the one used by AI in the Alliance cluster. Instead of working in schools, AI and congregations worked together to establish "academies" outside the schools to cultivate rela tionships between parents, teachers, and principals and provide them with information on educational issues.

Become a Voice in the Community

The above paragraphs provide the evidence that AI developed into a voice in the community to advocate for the policies that the constituent churches held and that were focused on improving conditions generally for the underserved and underrepresented in high-poverty, minority sections of Austin. By using the resources, both in terms of fees and developed leadership, to build bridges to other major organizations, such as the chamber of commerce, the teachers' association, the district, and the business community, AI became a voice for reform and argued effectively to policymakers. Clear successes included helping change the law on testing through providing repeated testimony throughout the state. The efforts described to develop better testing, by soliciting input from education and business leaders and drawing them together, allowed AI to speak for multiple parties on this issue to Texas legislatures. Working with business connections, it helped focus the business community on the issues that the undereducated faced and on how, without better educational opportunities, the state economy could not grow. At the time of our last visit, this effort was beginning to develop into a unified voice for change in Texas, and interviewees in the larger community credit AI as having played an important part in raising the level of discourse.

DC VOICE

DC VOICE's efforts during CERI 1 focused on providing professional development and other services to a cluster of schools in Northwest Washington. By the end of CERI 1, it had developed SQT, a series of policy supports that, if enacted, could lead to higher-quality teaching and learning. Its position was that the DCPS had strong standards and curriculum that were not being implemented because schools lacked basic supports (e.g., high-quality teachers and safe facilities that opened on time). The main policy domains included recruitment and hiring, new teacher induction, professional development, school-level administration, teaching and learning conditions, community involvement, and human resources. The policies it promoted were in keeping with the literature and the experiences of other, more-successful districts. For example, SQT included such policies as hiring teachers before the start of the school year, ensuring a diverse and well-qualified pool of teachers, ensuring positive induction experiences for new teachers, providing professional development and competitive salaries, and ensuring that the schools opened on time with safe, healthy, and adequate facilities and materials.

By the beginning of CERI 2, DC VOICE decided to advocate for SQT rather than provide professional development directly. In addition, it hoped to become a voice in the community, be recognized for promoting rational policies, and help community members become strong, research-based advocates.

Promote Policies That Lead to Quality in Teaching and Learning

Having developed SQT, in 2004, DC VOICE created flyers, handouts, and testimony on SQT that were distributed at public meetings and advocated for these supports. It convened yearly sessions in each ward (a political subdivision of the city) to facilitate discussions pertaining to public education among community members (including government officials, policymakers, researchers, and parents). DC VOICE used these sessions to share research findings and help community members identify and prioritize educational issues that their schools faced.

Early in CERI 2, DC VOICE started a major new initiative called the Ready Schools Project. In keeping with SQT principles, as well as the idea of being a research-based voice in the community, DC VOICE decided to investigate on an annual basis how ready the schools were to open each year. Note that the DCPS was known for opening with many teacher slots unfilled, buildings in poor repair, and textbooks missing. Thus, the focus made sense for the DCPS circumstances.

DC VOICE developed a principal survey to determine what supports were in place at the opening of the schools. The survey asked about such issues as teaching slots filled, textbooks ready, desks and other equipment in place, and facilities up to code. It trained more than 50 community volunteers to administer the surveys. The initial survey was administered to 43 schools in the fall of 2004, and the first Ready Schools Project report came out in early 2005. The report revealed more-serious deficits in readiness than reported by the DCPS administration.

In subsequent years, DC VOICE expanded the survey to more schools (from 43 to more than 130) and trained more volunteers. It also added more survey questions concerning professional development provision and wrap-around services that had been a key reform promise of the Fenty administration. It started a separate inquiry targeting schools being structured under No Child Left Behind and implemented a Ready Classroom Community Action Research Project beginning in school year 2008–2009. This project interviewed more than 116 teachers across every middle and high school about their instructional practices, relationships with the school administration and other teachers, and school climate.

Each year, DC VOICE has released the Ready Schools Project report (as well as others on specific issues), testified to the city council, and reported findings at town hall meetings.

DC VOICE has undertaken additional activities to inform policy, in partnership with other organizations. This collaboration has expanded the depth and reach of the organizations' work and produced reports on high schools (with Parents United), the state of DCPS facilities (with 21st Century), special education and the budget, and student achievement.

DC VOICE appeared to be well known by the different mayoral administrations and especially by actors associated with the city council through 2007. With the Fenty administration's takeover of the D.C. schools in 2007, DC VOICE had to establish new contacts. In addition, its director was replaced by a former board member. By 2008, the D.C. government was experiencing significant budget problems and closing schools. Throughout its history, DC VOICE has faced rapid changes in administrations and personnel and struggled to influence policy.

Become a Voice for the Community

After attending a CERI conference, the new director appeared more energized toward establishing DC VOICE as a voice for the underserved. Originally, DC VOICE appeared to be focused on educating the public at large and in disseminating neutral, research-based information to voters and decisionmakers. Recent efforts focused more on ensuring the development of leaders from underserved communities, including low-income, minority families from outside the northwest quadrant of the city, ensuring their participation in town hall meetings, and generally adopting community-organizing techniques to engage otherwise-underserved populations.

Although leaders in the community were aware of DC VOICE and especially of the Ready Schools Project Report, not all were highly supportive of the effort. For example, the city council, which oversees DCPS and has shown its lack of support for the mayor on many issues, questioned the validity of the more-recent Ready Schools findings, given countervailing evidence by the district. In early years, when DC VOICE focused on SQT, many interviewees discussed its impact on policies concerning induction and mentoring. Recent interviewees, however, expressed concern that DC VOICE had switched from being a neutral watchdog to advocacy. Others were less aware of its presence, which indicates that DC VOICE might have a diminishing role in the policy arena.

Grow Your Own

Low-quality teaching and high teacher turnover, especially in low-socioeconomic-status neighborhood schools, have been major challenges that public schools have faced in Chicago and across the nation. The major activity undertaken by GYO was the development and implementation of a GYO teacher pipeline in response to high rates of teacher turnover, shortages of teachers for hard-to-fill positions, and too few teachers who understood the culture, language, and community of the students they were teaching. It had few activities that were intended to directly affect teaching and learning in schools, other than through the pipeline or to create a voice in the community, so these areas are not covered here. We note, however, that all the partners have strong community-organizing functions and have consistently worked toward the goal of becoming a voice in their community for social reform.

Promote Policies That Lead to Quality in Teaching and Learning

The collaborative member organizations had job development missions, so targeting the working poor as teacher candidates was consistent with their missions to help increase economic opportunities in the neighborhoods they served. Collaborative members indicated that the design of the GYO teacher pipeline was informed by early data from a North Carolina program presented at the National Conference of State Legislatures and an evaluation of a Wallace Foundation initiative. The GYO design was modeled on the teacher-education programs of one of the collaborative partners, the LSNA. In 2000, the LSNA received a federal grant to target parents and school paraprofessionals in order to help them obtain their teaching credential and become bilingual-education teachers. The LSNA saw the program as addressing the need for more bilingual-education teachers in its service area and creating jobs for the working poor. At the time of this decision, the LSNA program outcomes had not been fully evaluated, but the collaborative perceived early results as being successful.

The collaborative drafted a state law based on the LSNA model to create a similar program statewide. GYO ran a strong campaign to bring the program to the attention of legislators. The collaborative members organized several advocacy efforts, sending representatives, including participants from the LSNA program, to the state capital to visit legislators and request support for the bill. These efforts were successful in getting support from the governor and legislature to pass the bill and enable appropriations. The purpose of Illinois Public Act 095-0476 is to "prepare highly skilled, committed teachers who will teach in hard-to-staff schools and hard-to-staff teaching positions and who will remain in these schools for substantial periods of time." The legislation indicates an expectation that the initiative will "increase the diversity of teachers including diversity based on race, ethnicity, and disability" (110 ILCS 48/5 Section 5).

This legislative approach provided GYO with political support from the governor and legislatures and supported a stream of state funding for implementation. The Illinois State Board of Education (ISBE) posted RFPs for grants for planning and implementing the GYO program. Each of the (then six) collaborative organizations wrote and won a planning grant to create a GYO initiative in their own neighborhoods with partners that included a four-year higher-education institution and CPS. The collaborative as a whole jointly and successfully wrote a proposal for a contract to help ISBE implement the pipeline statewide.

In many of the GYO consortia across the state, the partnership between the two- and four-year colleges had necessitated the development of articulation agreements to ensure that the courses taken at community college levels would be credited toward the degree at the higher-education institutions. Articulation agreements were not in place prior to the GYO pipeline, and the establishment of these agreements is a major legacy of the collaborative effort. Several institutions noted that they have gone on to establish further agreements of this type.

GYO was designed to recruit 1,000 teachers by 2016 (600 or more of those in Chicago) to supplement existing pipelines. However, this number would never be sufficient for CPS to meet its needs, let alone the state. CPS hires approximately 2,000 new teachers annually. Therefore, CPS and the state rely on other certification programs as sources for new teachers as well. In that respect, the GYO teacher pipeline was described by some school districts' human resource personnel and university partners as a small effort in comparison with existing traditional teacher pathways and other certification programs (e.g., Teach for America, Chicago Teaching Fellows, and Inner-City Teaching Corps).

By 2009, the 16 consortia that were established to implement the GYO pipeline had recruited only 545 teacher candidates across the state. Although the state provided funding each year, it did not allocate the full amount needed to meet the 1,000-candidate target. The consortia screened candidates, looking at academic readiness. About

60 percent entered with some college credits. Nevertheless, as part-time students who worked full time, the GYO teacher candidates were taking substantially more time to complete the program than traditional students. In 2009, about half of the candidates were taking developmental classes at the community colleges, and none had graduated from the program.[1] If the LSNA is any indication, it is estimated that it will take the GYO candidates an average of eight years (possibly more for teacher candidates with only a high school diploma) to graduate, as opposed to an average of five years for regular college students. As a result, program support structures, such as wrap-around services, will likely need to be maintained for that long, and the collaborative will have to look for additional funding sources or find ways to increase the state funding of the program.

Since teacher candidates have been taking longer to finish the degree, it can be expected that their dropout rate will be higher than in traditional programs. (GYO reported a dropout rate of 16 percent statewide; however, these numbers are underestimated because their calculations included replacement candidates.) The long-term impact of the GYO program will also depend on high retention rates over time as the GYO graduates stay in Chicago schools. In 2007, the collaborative started paying attention to this issue by exploring the status of high-quality teacher induction and mentorship programs in the public schools that will be hiring the GYO teachers. By the time of our visit, they still had not identified effective models to implement in GYO schools.

Cross-Site Themes on the Implementation of Activities

Our analysis of the major activities undertaken, their reasonableness, and implementation progress identifies several cross-cutting themes in CERI 2 sites.

---

[1]   GYO representatives claim that six candidates have graduated, but each of these came from the original LSNA program that started in 2000.

The Criteria Used for Choosing an Intervention Played a Large Role in Its Success

Our assessment of the reasonableness of the choices made showed that some sites chose activities that could not affect student achievement within the time frame of CERI 2, were not well coordinated, or were not appropriate for the needs of the students they intended to serve. The development of the teacher pipeline in Austin, dependent on subsidies from private higher-education institutions, was one such example. Respondents from institutions in Austin and Chicago noted that existing alternative programs targeted qualified applicants and moved them into the schools more quickly and at less cost than the process developed by the collaboratives.

Other activities chosen addressed the needs of the population or education sector, but the CBOs involved did not always consider what was feasible within the environment in which they operated or did not fully understand the challenges involved. The pursuit of an independent mini-district in Austin and the development of a fee-for-service model for progressive pedagogy in Puerto Rico are examples.

In contrast, several sites developed and implemented activities that made contributions within a short period of time: the set of counseling and college-access activities in Jackson; the Principal's Council in Jackson; the changes in state testing laws in Texas; improvements in induction and mentoring in the District of Columbia; and the creation and continuing implementation of the Ready Schools project in the District of Columbia. Common to these initiatives are a focus on a very specific issue in which research could be used to highlight its importance to policymakers, a specific solution that could be constructed within the existing policy time frame, limited costs associated with implementation, and an advocacy role well within the capabilities of the organizations involved. In some cases, the impact was far reaching. The change in state law concerning testing time in Texas, for example, had an immediate impact on children throughout the state.

Regular Needs Assessment and Reflection Enabled Beneficial Adaptation of Interventions

The implementation of any intervention or activity can be threatened by unforeseen conditions. The sites that regularly evaluated and analyzed their strategies tended to identify what was or was not working and why, and then made adjustments accordingly. For example, after a year of attempting to establish Alliance schools to improve school performance, AI realized that its approach was failing and straining relationships with the district. AI decided to adopt a community-mobilization strategy to affect local policy instead. AI's leadership played a critical role in encouraging and facilitating the process of reflection. DC VOICE, facing continuously changing circumstances within the district, adopted this approach early on and continued to use it for specific issues, such as how to improve the Ready Schools Project on an annual basis and to assess and improve its fund-raising and board activities.

Use of Collaborative Approaches to Implementation Facilitated Progress

Sites that used collaborative approaches tended to progress further in implementing activities to affect teaching and learning. AI, for example, sought out various types of influential organizations and congregations and involved them in its efforts as equal partners. AI and its partners worked jointly together on several efforts related to education policy, including advocating for legislation. This resulted in stronger stakeholder support and better implementation of these efforts, as well as better outcomes, as evidenced by the passage of a bill designed to reduce the amount of time schools can spend assessing students.

In contrast, DC VOICE moved away from its collaborative approach to forming short-term partnerships with many small CBOs. Similarly, GYO did not always cultivate collaborative and equal partnerships between the CBOs and the colleges, which hindered relationships with some of the consortium members.

Collaboratives Faced Challenges in Implementing Activities with Dwindling Foundation Support

Similar to findings from the last chapter, we found that CERI 2 supported some projects that could be considered overly ambitious in relation to their funding. Two collaboratives, AI and GYO, consisted of well-established organizations with traditional sources of funding that they were able to tap for support. However, three grantees, the Alianza, AFM, and DC VOICE, were created specifically for CERI from organizations with less-established funding streams and in cities with few local philanthropic resources. In fact, early briefings from RAND noted that securing funding for these three collaboratives would be a potential issue (Bodilly, Chun, et al., 2004).

DC VOICE dedicated significant efforts to raising funds and successfully brought in several grants to continue its work. However, AFM was not able to do this. It did apply for and was successful in securing grant funding for the Ford arts initiative. However, this switched its focus in the last two years toward arts integration and diminished work on CERI 2 activities.

The Alianza faced even more challenges because it did not have a focused set of activities. Its growth in CERI 1 to a provider model left it ill equipped to deal with dwindling resources later. Its dependence on the Ford Foundation left it with few options in the final years as the foundation sector was hit with a recession.

Thus, a major barrier to the implementation of the activities was the lack of funding to carry them forward. This was most pronounced for those grantees with organizations that were highly dependent on the CERI funds. However, as one respondent argued,

> While funding was an issue in the context of where we are situated, there is always a need to do more with less—it is an understood phenomenon in this area. So strategic and intentional focus is the only way to bridge the lean times.

Several of the sites were braced for these times and selectively chose which initiatives to pursue during the lean years.

Intervention Implementation Was Affected by the Political and Economic Context

We do not know what will happen to the grantees as they navigate the economic recession. But the economy and political forces certainly influenced several in their attempts to implement their sets of activities. The Alianza and AFM were particularly hit by external influences. In Puerto Rico, the growing unrest and budget crisis resulted in the failure of the fee-for-service model, as well as dwindling support for the ministry's five model initiatives, which would have allowed the Alianza to grow. In Jackson, changes to the superintendent's office and the board meant less overt support for AFM activities. In Illinois, GYO's dependence on state funds during a major fiscal downturn resulted in an inability to meet proposed goals for scale-up.

CHAPTER FIVE

Conclusions and Observations

The purpose of our study was to answer three broad questions:

1. Did grantees show progress toward desired outcomes?
2. What lessons or promising practices result from the experiences of individual collaboratives or groups of grantees?
3. Did the initiative create financially sustainable collaboratives that can promote education improvement?

In this chapter, we summarize findings and conclusions, especially answering the third research question, and offer some observations for future efforts.

Findings and Conclusions

As illustrated in Chapters Three and Four, creating successful and sustainable collaboratives in local communities is a challenging endeavor. AI became a well-functioning collaborative with significant interorganizational linkages at both the local and state levels. It showed significant capability to sustain itself independent of the foundation. In general, the remaining sites experienced less growth in terms of collaboration and financial sustainability, or exhibited a weakening of and stasis in interorganizational linkages and collaborative power at the end of the initiative, which, in part, reflects the end date of the work in the midst of a major recession.

With respect to the activities in which the collaboratives engaged, the selection of interventions, degree of implementation, and the extent to which the interventions promoted teaching and learning varied among sites. However, irrespective of the type of intervention and level of implementation, the expected impact of selected interventions on school and student performance was not empirically evident at the point of the last visit. Most of the selected interventions were unlikely to have a direct effect on teaching and learning in classrooms, while interventions developed in Jackson were likely to have effects on attainment if well implemented and maintained.

Our study found that four of the five grantees were able to affect local and state policies related to teaching and learning, relying heavily on community-organizing approaches described by Shirley (1997) and Warren (2001). The effects that these new policies will have on actual school performance remain unquantifiable. Finally, one of the grantees (AI) was successful in becoming a strong voice for reform at both the local and state levels. AFM and DC VOICE also developed strong voices for reform; these collaboratives targeted more-specific local issues, and their reach did not extend beyond the local communities.

Turning to lessons learned from this effort, we identified a number of themes that emerged across sites. These lessons represent a pattern of findings about "what matters" that could be instructive for future efforts intended to create and sustain collaboratives dedicated to improving public education. These themes should also be useful to funders that support or intend to support such efforts, as well as to the CERI 2 grantees as they continue with their collaborative efforts. We summarize these lessons learned in three sections: building and sustaining collaboratives, promoting quality in teaching and learning, and developing a voice for reform.

Building and Sustaining Collaboratives

Two of the foundation's premises for promoting collaboratives were based on the assertions that (1) the central office lacks constancy of vision due to political instability and lack of stakeholder buy-in and (2) central-office inputs, such as funding for initiatives, are unreliable. Our study found that community-based collaboratives were also vulnerable to these same phenomena and conditions. The grantees' ability (or, in some cases, inability) to build strong collaboratives and sustain them could be traced to leadership turnover, funding constraints, and instability in the political system within which the collaboratives are embedded. Other factors that proved to be important were

- the strength and style of leadership in collaborative building
- the perceived legitimacy of not just the lead organization but also other members of the collaborative
- the manner in which collaborative members worked together
    - the ability to build bridges across collaborative members with different or larger missions
    - the ability to share information and engage in shared decisionmaking
- the willingness to be reflective and adjust strategies as a result of changes in context
- early attention to sustaining the collaborative by securing future sources of funds.

Promoting Quality in Teaching and Learning

The foundation also justified the need to involve CBOs to promote teaching and learning based on its observation that district leaders often make poor choices for reform and lack the ability to implement innovative solutions. Our study found that collaboratives were similarly challenged. The collaboratives in our study did not always select interventions proven to affect school improvement and student learning (at least, not in the short term of the CERI grants). However, our research indicated that the collaboratives were able to influence reform from the "outside" with varying degrees of progress, depending on their relationships with the district and the strength of stakeholder support. For example, AFM's principal collaborative led to new practices in the district. Similarly, AI's mobilizing effort resulted in changing policies pertaining to student assessment at both the local and state levels. Other factors that were important in order for collaboratives to promote teaching and learning, at least for this initiative, were

- the adoption of interventions that were proven to be effective and aligned with identified educational goals and contextual needs and conditions
- the selection of interventions that were aligned with collaboratives' expertise and capabilities
- the availability of expertise and willingness to conduct needs assessment on a regular basis to examine whether the interventions were performing as intended
- the use of collaborative approaches in implementing interventions.

Developing a Voice for Reform

The difference in the sites' progress for gaining a voice within their communities was highly influenced by the political context and the developing nature of the movement itself. Both DC VOICE's and AFM's efforts to expand their reach to a wider audience were hindered, partly a result of the rapid leadership changes in the central district and mayoral offices, while both organizations were themselves developing. Furthermore, they were just learning about this type of organizing. Both sites spent much of their energy cultivating new relationships and identifying new audiences for addressing education issues. The political context in Austin was fairly stable, allowing AI to establish long-term relationships at both the local and state levels. We note that these relationships were established long before the CERI grant and that AI had a strong reputation for community organizing in the Austin area prior to the initiative. Other factors that were identified as important for creating a constituency voice were

- consistency of and adherence to the collaborative mission over time to strengthen public confidence in collaborative work
- the involvement of a broad segment of the community, including a wide range of leaders and organizations that have legitimacy and power in the education policy arena.

Emerging Lessons for Foundation Efforts

Our findings indicated that CERI showed promise in encouraging collaboration among different community organizations but could not ensure collaborative sustainability. CERI funding provided an opportunity, otherwise not readily available, for CBOs to collaborate with each other on improving K–12 public education. The foundation made it possible for grantees to develop networks, to share information, and to act cooperatively with each other on educational issues. Most importantly, it allowed the sites to choose their own interventions and learn from their own mistakes. By engaging in these activities, the grantees learned how to collaborate and, in several instances, extended these collaborations into new efforts not related to the foundation's initiative.

Although, at one point in time, all five sites had formed strong collaborative linkages, sustaining these linkages and maintaining a focus on education-improvement efforts proved to be challenging. Our data suggest that there are several ways in which the foundation might have missed important opportunities to help the sites by providing more financial support and by being more involved throughout CERI. Although we separately detail here five actions the foundation might have taken, we note that, taken in concert, they would likely have had stronger impact. In short, greater funding by itself would not have necessarily propelled the sites forward, but, combined with clear goals and greater technical support, it might have proved more beneficial.

First, the foundation might have provided more monies to the sites. On average, each site was awarded about $300,000 for each year of CERI 2. A portion of the funds was to be used for the development of the collaboratives and not only interventions. The lack of sufficient resources limited the choices of interventions in which the sites could reasonably engage. Or, alternatively, the foundation's goals for CERI might have contributed to sites' choices of overly ambitious goals that could not be supported by the available Ford funding. Other sources would be needed, and the fiscal environment at the end of the CERI grant period was not conducive to obtaining grants from other foundations for work they had not sponsored.

Second, the foundation might have provided greater clarity about the goals and objectives of CERI 2. In general, the foundation adopted an ambitious but general set of goals, while using a "hands-off" approach, allowing the sites to define their own more-specific educational goals and outcomes and to determine the appropriate interventions. As a result, many of the long-term goals identified by the sites were either too ambitious or too marginal, and the interventions, in many instances, were not aligned with the intended outcomes.

Third, the foundation could have provided stronger management support to ensure that the grantees thoroughly considered their goals and interventions. Specifically, the sites could have benefited from additional technical assistance, especially in their planning year. While technical support had been provided in CERI 1, such support was largely missing in CERI 2. Without ongoing technical support, foundation personnel had to review the sites' identification of the problems, goals, intervention choices, and activities with a skeptical eye, asking probing questions about the probability of impact. This came at a time when the foundation was reorganizing and its staff in this area shrinking. Although RAND and LCN raised concerns about some of the choices, these concerns did not result in any change in directions by grantees or the foundation.

Fourth, the foundation might have provided the sites with training in grant writing and fundraising to facilitate the collaboratives' move toward financial sustainment. It might also have encouraged grantees to gather data on the expected or actual impact of their interventions— such evidence can be used to make a stronger case to potential funders. However, the foundation did not emphasize the need to link interventions to outcomes or require the sites to collect such information.

Finally, the foundation might have encouraged convenings and data sharing among the sites on a more-regular basis. Such activities are useful because they can help sites learn from each other about progress and they can help motivate the sites' interest and energy in their efforts.

Although these lessons apply to foundations, we also think they apply to the collaborative sites. In particular, we identify the following as important considerations for sites undertaking collaborative efforts:

- Sites should be thoughtful in aligning their goals, their chosen interventions, and the available funding source with the expectations for progress within the time frame provided. More thought, information gathering, and more-deliberative processes for exploring a theory of change might lead sites to effective choices.
- Sites should focus attention early on to the eventual need for future fund raising. In our sample, the earlier this was attended to, the more successfully the site ensured steady resources.
- Sites consistently overlooked the difficulties of collaboration, especially those that were forming as organizations at the same time as they were building a reform agenda. Both sites and foundations might consider the participation of more-established partners to help relieve the burden of developing organizationally, collaboratively, and in reform experience all at the same time. An extraordinary amount of effort and learning took place in these sites over the past five years. Perhaps this steep incline might have been reduced had more-mature CBOs been part of some of the efforts.
- Finally, this work and the literature point to processes that collaboratives adopt to ensure progress, including data gathering, collaborative decisionmaking, sharing of information, and the development of joint goals and actions. New collaborative efforts can easily take advantage of this literature to help ensure smoother and more-effective functioning.

It is important to point out that adopting these suggestions might not guarantee stronger, more-successful collaboratives. Adopting them could, however, equip the sites to overcome some of the hurdles they faced. Thus, foundations that are engaged in promoting collaborative approaches to reform might want to ensure the provision of concrete support and guidance to CBOs to help them assess their environment and capabilities, identify appropriate goals, and choose "reasonable" interventions that are linked to goals. It is also critical for foundations to adopt and communicate a systematic approach to a theory of change and for sites to commit to such processes. More up-front discussion, planning, and critical review by both parties could help identify flaws and the revisions needed early on and perhaps contribute to the success of collaborative efforts.

That being said, a respondent summed up her experiences this way:

> Yes, a little more direction may have helped. Certainly, a bit more money would have helped. However, we were allowed to make mistakes and grow and build on them. The lessons we learned and the space we were given to learn and act on them were invaluable. We know that, without Ford Foundation's support throughout this effort, we would not have been able to sustain and grow this work over these many years.

References

Baker, Linda M., "Promoting Success in Educational Partnerships Involving Technology," in *Proceedings of Selected Research and Development Presentations at the Convention of the Association for Educational Communications and Technology, Sponsored by the Research and Theory Division*, New Orleans, La., January 13–17, 1993.

Berman, Paul, Peter W. Greenwood, Milbrey Wallin McLaughlin, and John A. Pincus, *Federal Programs Supporting Educational Change*, Vol. IV (Abridged): *A Summary of the Findings in Review*, Santa Monica, Calif.: RAND Corporation, R-1589/13-HEW, 1975. As of December 9, 2010: http://www.rand.org/pubs/reports/R1589z13.html

Bodilly, Susan J., JoAn Chun, Gina Schuyler Ikemoto, and Sue Stockly, *Challenges and Potential of a Collaborative Approach to Education Reform*, Santa Monica, Calif.: RAND Corporation, MG-216-FF, 2004. As of December 9, 2010: http://www.rand.org/pubs/monographs/MG216.html

Bodilly, Susan J., with Brent R. Keltner, Susanna W. Purnell, Robert Reichardt, and Gina Schuyler Ikemoto, *Lessons from New American Schools' Scale-Up Phase: Prospects for Bringing Designs to Multiple Schools*, Santa Monica, Calif.: RAND Corporation, MR-942-NAS, 1998. As of December 9, 2010: http://www.rand.org/pubs/monograph_reports/MR942.html

Cuban, Larry, "Transforming the Frog into a Prince: Effective Schools Research, Policy, and Practice at the District Level," *Harvard Educational Review*, Vol. 54, No. 2, May 1984, pp. 129–151.

Daft, R., "Bureaucratic Versus Non-Bureaucratic Structure and the Process of Innovation and Change," *Research in the Sociology of Organizations*, Vol. 1, 1982, pp. 129–166.

Dluhy, Milan J., *Building Coalitions in the Human Services*, Newbury Park, Calif.: Sage Publications, 1990.

———, "Request for Proposals: Collaborating for Educational Reform Initiative," New York: Ford Foundation, 1997.

————, "Request for Proposals: Collaborating for Educational Reform," New York: Ford Foundation, 1999.

————, *Ford Foundation Annual Report, 2001*, New York: Ford Foundation, 2002.

Gitlin, Andrew, and Frank Margonis, "The Political Aspect of Reform: Teacher Resistance as Good Sense," *American Journal of Education*, Vol. 103, No. 4, August 1995, pp. 377–405.

Himmelman, Arthur Turovh, *Communities Working Collaboratively for a Change*, Minneapolis, Minn.: Himmelman Consulting Group, 1996.

Hogue, Teresa, "Community Based Collaborations—Wellness Multiplied," Oregon Center for Community Leadership, 1994.

Huberman, A. Michael, and Matthew B. Miles, "Rethinking the Quest for School Improvement: Some Findings from the DESSI Study," *Teachers College Record*, Vol. 86, No. 1, Fall 1984, pp. 34–54.

Iwanowsky, J., "Can Partnering Succeed? You Betcha," *Business Officer*, September 1996.

Kaganoff, Tessa, *Collaboration, Technology, and Outsourcing Initiatives in Higher Education: A Literature Review*, Santa Monica, Calif.: RAND Corporation, MR-973-EDU, 1998. As of December 9, 2010: http://www.rand.org/pubs/monograph_reports/MR973.html

Keith, Joanne, *Building and Maintaining Community Coalitions on Behalf of Children, Youth and Families: Community Coalitions in Action, Institute for Children, Youth, and Families*, East Lansing, Mich.: Michigan State University, Agricultural Experiment Station, 1993.

Lieberman, Ann, and Milbrey W. McLaughlin, "Networks for Educational Change: Powerful and Problematic," *Phi Delta Kappan*, Vol. 73, No. 9, May 1992, pp. 673–677.

Marsh, Julie A., *Democratic Dilemmas: Joint Work, Education Politics, and Community*, dissertation, Stanford, Calif.: Stanford University, 2002.

Mattessich, Paul W., and Barbara R. Monsey, *Collaboration: What Makes It Work—A Review of Research Literature on Factors Influencing Successful Collaboration*, St. Paul, Minn.: Amherst H. Wilder Foundation, 1992.

Mazmanian, Daniel A., and Paul A. Sabatier, *Implementation and Public Policy, with a New Postscript*, Lanham, Md.: University Press of America, 1989.

McDonnell, Lorraine M., and W. Norton Grubb, *Education and Training for Work: The Policy Instruments and the Institutions*, Santa Monica, Calif.: RAND Corporation, R-4026-NCRVE/UCB, 1991. As of December 9, 2010: http://www.rand.org/pubs/reports/R4026.html

McLaughlin, Milbrey Wallin, "Learning from Experience: Lessons from Policy Implementation," *Educational Evaluation and Policy Analysis*, Vol. 9, No. 2, Summer 1987, pp. 171–178.

———, "The RAND Change Agent Study Revisited: Macro Perspectives and Micro Realities," *Educational Researcher*, Vol. 19, No. 9, December 1990, pp. 11–16.

Melaville, Atelia I., and Martin J. Blank, *What It Takes: Structuring Interagency Partnerships to Connect Children and Families with Comprehensive Services*, Washington, D.C.: Education and Human Services Consortium, 1991.

Pressman, Jeffrey L., and Aaron B. Wildavsky, Implementation: *How Great Expectations in Washington Are Dashed in Oakland; Or, Why It's Amazing That Federal Programs Work at All, This Being a Saga of the Economic Development Administration as Told by Two Sympathetic Observers Who Seek to Build Morals on a Foundation of Ruined Hopes*, Berkeley, Calif.: University of California Press, 1973.

Public Law 107-110, No Child Left Behind Act of 2001, January 8, 2002.

School Communities That Work, *Developing Effective Partnerships to Support Local Education*, Providence, R.I.: Annenberg Institute for School Reform, Brown University, 2002. As of December 9, 2010:
http://www.annenberginstitute.org/products/EffectivePartnerships.php

Shirley, Dennis, *Community Organizing for Urban School Reform*, Austin, Texas: University of Texas Press, 1997.

Stone, Clarence N., ed., *Changing Urban Education*, Lawrence, Kan.: University Press of Kansas, 1998.

Warren, Mark R., *Dry Bones Rattling: Community Building to Revitalize American Democracy*, Princeton, N.J.: Princeton University Press, 2001.

Weatherley, Richard, and Michael Lipsky, "Street-Level Bureaucrats and Institutional Innovation: Implementing Special-Education Reform," *Harvard Educational Review*, Vol. 47, No. 2, 1977, pp. 171–197.

Wenger, Etienne, *Communities of Practice: Learning, Meaning, and Identity*, Cambridge, UK: Cambridge University Press, 1998.

Winer, Michael Barry, and Karen Louise Ray, *Collaboration Handbook: Creating, Sustaining, and Enjoying the Journey*, Saint Paul, Minn.: Amherst H. Wilder Foundation, 1994.

Yin, Robert K., *Changing Urban Bureaucracies: How New Practices Become Routinized*, Lexington, Mass.: Lexington Books, 1979.

Project AIR FORCE

ORGANIZATIONAL POLICY LEVERS CAN AFFECT ACQUISITION REFORM IMPLEMENTATION IN AIR FORCE REPAIR CONTRACTS

Mary E. Chenoweth

Sarah Hunter

Brent Keltner

David Adamson

Prepared for the
UNITED STATES AIR FORCE

RAND

The research reported here was sponsored by the United States Air Force under Contract F49642-01-C-0003. Further information may be obtained from the Strategic Planning Division, Directorate of Plans, Hq USAF.

Library of Congress Cataloging-in-Publication Data

Organizational policy levers can affect acquisition reform implementation in Air Force repair contracts / Mary E. Chenoweth ... [et al.].
    p. cm.
    "MR-1711."
    Includes bibliographical references and index.
    ISBN 0-8330-3488-X (pbk. : alk. paper)
    1. Defense contracts—United States. 2. United States. Air Force—Procurement.
3. Airplanes, Military—United States—Maintenance and repair. I. Chenoweth,
Mary E.

UG1123.O73 2003
359.6'212—dc22

                                        2003021659

The RAND Corporation is a nonprofit research organization providing objective analysis and effective solutions that address the challenges facing the public and private sectors around the world. RAND's publications do not necessarily reflect the opinions of its research clients and sponsors.

RAND® is a registered trademark.

Published 2004 by the RAND Corporation
1700 Main Street, P.O. Box 2138, Santa Monica, CA 90407-2138
1200 South Hayes Street, Arlington, VA 22202-5050
201 North Craig Street, Suite 202, Pittsburgh, PA 15213-1516
RAND URL: http://www.rand.org/
To order RAND documents or to obtain additional information, contact
Distribution Services: Telephone: (310) 451-7002;
Fax: (310) 451-6915; Email: order@rand.org

This report describes a study of the implementation of innovative practices in Air Force depot maintenance contracts. Through its Contract Repair Enhancement Program (CREP), today known as the Contract Repair Process (CRP), the U.S. Air Force has encouraged contracting personnel to formulate more innovative contracts aimed at improving contractors' performance, particularly regarding cost and schedule. Successful implementation of this reform requires a transformation in organizational structures and processes because implementation requires individuals to change fundamental business practices. This study focused on the relationship between organizational levers—those aspects of the work environment that senior leadership could affect to encourage personnel to implement reform—and contract innovation. These organizational levers were measured through a survey of contracting personnel at Warner Robins Air Logistics Center (ALC). Next, the study team designed a set of regression models to examine whether these levers were related to innovation in repair contracts.

The research reported here is one element of the RAND Corporation's ongoing work on improved contracting sponsored by the Office of the Secretary of the Air Force, Deputy Assistant Secretary for Contracting (SAF/AQC). The study was conducted in the Resource Management Program of RAND Project AIR FORCE.

This report may be of interest to those concerned with acquisition reform improvements to Air Force repair contracts, organizational transformation, and implementation of acquisition reform contracting practices.

In the last decade, RAND Project AIR FORCE has been helping the Air Force reshape its sourcing policies and practices. Readers may also be interested in the following related reports:

- *Implementing Best Purchasing and Supply Management Practices: Lessons from Innovative Commercial Firms*, Nancy Y. Moore, Laura H. Baldwin, Frank Camm, and Cynthia Cook, RAND, DB-334-AF, 2002, which can be downloaded from www.rand.org/publications/DB/DB334.

- *Implementing Performance-Based Services Acquisition (PBSA): Perspectives from an Air Logistics Center and a Product Center*, John Ausink, Laura H. Baldwin, Sarah Hunter, and Chad Shirley, RAND, DB-388-AF, 2002, which can be downloaded from www.rand.org/publications/DB/DB388.

- *Federal Contract Bundling: A Framework for Making and Justifying Decisions for Purchased Services*, Laura H. Baldwin, Frank Camm, and Nancy Y. Moore, RAND, MR-1224-AF, 2001, which can be downloaded from www.rand.org/publications/ MR/MR1224.

- *Performance-Based Contracting in the Air Force: A Report on Experiences in the Field*, John Ausink, Frank Camm, and Charles Cannon, RAND, DB-342-AF, 2001, which can be downloaded from www.rand.org/publications/DB/DB342.

- *Strategic Sourcing: Measuring and Managing Performance*, Laura H. Baldwin, Frank Camm, and Nancy Y. Moore, RAND, DB-287-AF, 2000, which can be downloaded from www.rand.org/ publications/DB/DB287.

- *Incentives to Undertake Sourcing Studies in the Air Force*, Laura H. Baldwin, Frank Camm, Edward Keating, and Ellen M. Pint, RAND, DB-240-AF, 1998.

- *Strategic Sourcing: Theory and Evidence from Economics and Business Management*, Ellen M. Pint and Laura H. Baldwin, RAND, MR-865-AF, 1997.

RAND PROJECT AIR FORCE

RAND Project AIR FORCE (PAF), a division of the RAND Corporation, is the Air Force federally funded research and development center for studies and analyses. PAF provides the Air Force with independent analyses of policy alternatives affecting the development, employment, combat readiness, and support of current and future aerospace forces. Research is performed in four programs: Aerospace Force Development; Manpower, Personnel, and Training; Resource Management; and Strategy and Doctrine.

Additional information about PAF may be found on our web site at http://www.rand.org/paf.

CONTENTS

FIGURES

TABLES

In 1996, the Air Force adopted the Contract Repair Enhancement Program (CREP), today known as the Contract Repair Process (CRP), which consisted of a series of contracting reform measures intended to respond directly to customer demands at the same time as reducing inventory, process steps, lead time, and total system operating costs. Further, the Air Force aimed to accomplish these reform measures while maintaining or improving readiness. These new practices were modeled on earlier Air Force changes in acquisition practices that led to cost improvements and accelerated program schedules for acquiring major weapon systems. Concerned by what appeared to be the initially slow pace at which depot personnel were carrying out the CREP reforms, the Air Force asked RAND to assess what might be hindering their implementation.

PURPOSE AND APPROACH

In the Air Force, as in the private sector, senior leadership plays a vital role in instigating change in business practices. To do so, leaders generally use a range of tools, or *organizational levers*, designed to motivate personnel. Such levers might include setting new goals and objectives, communicating them throughout all levels of the organization, and changing performance evaluation and incentives in order to encourage their adoption. Particular to the set of reform measures that the Air Force planned to undertake was increased teaming among personnel. Similarly, success at the operating level, which is where most repair contracts are written, depends on how effectively senior leadership can move personnel toward continued use of new practices after their initial introduction. The authors analyzed whether the Air Force's existing *organizational levers* resulted in the use of CREP's innovative reforms within depot-level repair contracts. We focused on Warner Robins Air Logistics Center (ALC) because it had aggressively pursued the incorporation of CREP tenets in its repair contracts. It appeared that Warner Robins represented the ALC most likely to have the largest sample size and most variation in the number of CREP tenets incorporated in repair contracts.

Our study used a three-step approach. Step one consisted of a *literature review* on organizational levers and innovation in the private sector, combined with *interviews* with personnel considered to have excelled at incorporating CREP tenets in the first CREP contracts. The literature review and interviews formed the basis for step two, *a survey* of key personnel participating on contract repair teams (CRTs), i.e., program managers, procurement contracting officers, production management specialists, and item management specialists. Step three involved regression analyses. The survey was used to measure organizational levers, which became the independent variables. Survey data were used in combination with reported CREP tenets—the dependent variables—in the regression analyses. CREP tenets were classified by tenet groups—simple modifications, key acquisition reform concepts, complete acquisition reform concepts, agile logistics, and all CREP tenets—which became the dependent variables. Regression analyses were carried out to determine the relationship between each organizational lever and the number of CREP tenets incorporated in the contract. Each step is discussed in more detail below.

Literature Review and Interviews

In step one, we reviewed the business and management science literature on the kinds of organizational levers senior leadership uses to motivate private-sector enterprises to adopt new business practices. The literature review helped to identify organizational levers to be measured in the personnel survey. In turn, the review helped structure our subsequent interviews with CREP contracting teams at Warner Robins ALC. Similarly, the interviews helped us understand how these levers operated within the ALC and the CREP initiative and influenced the development of the next phase, the survey. We asked CRT personnel to talk about specific CREP contracts and asked them questions related to organizational levers within these examples of contract innovation. The interviews helped us to develop questions using language and context we believed were likely to resonate with potential survey participants, thus preparing us for step two.

Survey Development and Administration

In step two, based on inputs from the literature review and interviews conducted at Warner Robins ALC, we created a survey instrument designed to gather information on organizational levers. The survey asked questions in five categories that supplied data for eight organizational lever variables. Those categories were (1) attitude toward acquisition reform, (2) leadership support, (3) performance evaluation and rewards, (4) teaming and partnering, and (5) training and career development. We surveyed key members of contract repair teams. The survey was conducted first in 1998 and again in 1999 for only those participants who had missing data in the first round or failed to respond. Each participant provided only one set of responses.

Analyses

In step three, regression analyses showed that there was a relationship between organizational levers and reported CREP tenet use. Between December 1996 and September 1998, for each CREP contract, the ALCs considered the incorporation of 16 tenets identified by HQ Air Force Materiel Command (AFMC) as innovative and consistent with CREP goals. These reported tenets were used as the measure of contract innovation. The research process involved survey data, i.e., organizational levers that served as independent variables in the regression. The process also involved tenet data, which served as dependent variables in the regression analyses.

Step 3A.   Prior to the regression analyses, *Principal Components Analysis (PCA) was used to organize responses to organizational levers (the independent variables).* PCA allows the analyst to examine relationships among item responses to determine whether particular questions reflect the same underlying concept. The survey contained questions on organizational lever themes; thus, PCA provided a technique to group questions along these themes. The PCA technique helped identify eight organizational levers that were called:

- Attitude toward acquisition reform
- Leadership consistency
- Performance evaluation
- Performance incentives
- Effective teaming
- Contractor partnering
- Air Force partnering
- Training in acquisition reform.

Two other variables, job experience and a U-2 dummy variable for the U-2 Product Directorate, since renamed the Intelligence, Surveillance, and Reconnaissance Management Directorate, were computed directly and did not require PCA.

Step 3B. CREP Tenet Groups (the dependent variables). The study used CREP tenets as an element of the dependent variables, which were defined by AFMC as its measure of contract innovation and collected throughout the initiative. We received a record of the tenets Warner Robins ALC incorporated in their CREP contracts from HQ AFMC. Individual CREP tenets were not used as dependent variables, because they lacked policy significance by themselves. The question became one of how to group CREP tenets in ways that would have strategic policy relevance to decisionmakers, i.e., to high-level policy goals and objectives. We analyzed the tenet data using cluster analysis to discern the natural groups of tenets, but the cluster analysis showed tenet clusters that had no policy relevance. In the end, we chose to use as dependent variables groups of CREP tenets that were broadly defined by the CREP initiative itself and had strategic policy relevance, plus a fifth group that included all CREP tenets. Some tenets were included in more than one group.

The first innovation group, called *simple modifications*, included the easiest tenets to implement with still-active contracts, usually related to speeding up transportation. The second group, called *key acqui-*

sition reform concepts, consisted of reform tenets that were consistent with acquisition reform goals and could be measured more objectively. The third group, called *complete acquisition reform concepts*, measured all reform tenets included in the second group, plus other acquisition reform-related tenets that involved subjective measures. The fourth group, called *agile logistics*, included all tenets designed to reduce logistics pipelines by speeding up the repair and transportation pipeline segments, as well as improving other logistics efficiencies. The fifth group, called *all tenets*, included the complete set of CREP tenets. These five groups of tenets became the dependent variables.

Step 3C. Regression Analyses. We conducted five separate regression analyses to determine the relationship between the organizational levers used at Warner Robins and the incorporation of CREP tenets in repair contracts, designed to improve total weapon system costs and readiness. The regression analyses showed that some organizational levers help explain the incorporation of CREP tenets in repair contracts. Thus, this study demonstrated that senior leadership can influence contract innovation through organizational levers, although not always in expected ways. (See pp. 37–43.)

RESULTS: ORGANIZATIONAL LEVERS RELATED TO CONTRACT INNOVATION

Our analyses showed that organizational levers help explain the degree of tenet use that teams achieve with repair and sustainment contracts. The tenets ranged from easy-to-implement transportation improvements to more difficult acquisition reform measures, such as early contractor involvement in the contracting process. In some areas, the levers were positively related to the use of CREP tenets; in others, the levers were negative; and in a few, they had no influence at all. The findings were as follows:

- **Training in acquisition reform** had a consistent and positive statistical relationship with tenet use. The statistical analyses showed significance in all four groups of CREP tenets along with the group of all CREP tenets. CRT personnel who receive more training used more tenets in their contracts compared with personnel with less training. (See p. 38.)

- **Attitude toward acquisition reform** also had a consistent, positive statistical relationship on reported tenet use in all tenet groups, except as it related to key acquisition reform. These results suggest that contract teams that view reform more positively or agree with the goals of the initiative also implement more reform tenets in their contracts. (See p. 40.)

- **Effective teaming** had a negative statistical relationship with reported tenet use. Contract teams that reported effective teaming also implemented fewer tenets. (See p. 38.)

- **Contractor partnering** had a positive statistical relationship with simple modifications and agile logistics innovation goals. CRTs that perceived contractors to be better partners included more CREP tenets in their contracts. This result, however, did not occur with either of the two acquisition reform tenet models. (See p. 40.)

- **Leadership consistency** had a positive statistical relationship with tenet implementation. CRTs that perceived consistent messages throughout management and believed reform would be around for some time incorporated more agile logistics tenets in their contracts. (See pp. 40–41.)

- **Performance evaluation** had a surprisingly negative statistical relationship on CRT behavior with respect to agile logistics tenets and no significant relationship elsewhere. (See p. 41.)

- **Job experience** had a slight negative statistical relationship with the simple modifications and the complete acquisition reform innovation groups, but the magnitude was so minimal as to have little practical consequence.

Two variables—**performance incentives** and **Air Force partnering**—had no explanatory power in our analyses. Perhaps the types of incentives we included in the survey were not sufficiently representative of rewards offered or perhaps personnel do not perceive these rewards as effective. The lack of a relationship between Air Force partnering and the incorporation of CREP tenets, however, raises questions about the Air Force's view of itself as a customer and its effect on innovation.

Finally, we also tested a dummy variable that took into account different contracting processes and contracts that occurred in the **U-2 Product Directorate** (now the Intelligence, Surveillance, and Reconnaissance, or ISR Management Directorate). Specifically, the U-2 Product Directorate produced sustainment contracts that included repair services rather than solely repair contracts. Our analysis found that the fact that a contract was written at the U-2 Product Directorate was positively associated with the reported incorporation of complete acquisition reform concepts and agile logistics tenets in CREP contracts. At the time of this study, the U-2 Product Directorate reported a high rate of tenet use, which has been substantiated with follow up discussions at Warner Robins ALC.

LESSONS FOR THE AIR FORCE

In general, the results suggest that the Air Force should continue to make effective use of those levers associated with positive results (especially training and fostering positive attitudes toward acquisition reform), while revisiting others associated with negative results (especially performance evaluation and teaming). Specifically, the Air Force could do more to:

- Let personnel know that senior leadership wants to see progress in achieving well-specified contracting goals

- Learn how to create effective teams. This process will require training in group problem-solving and working with others from different functional backgrounds, in addition to educating teams on legal and policy changes

- Align personal evaluation criteria with reform goals.

EXTENDING THESE RESULTS TO OTHER ALCS AND INITIATIVES

To the degree that the CREP initiative is representative of contract reform efforts in general, the Air Force should consider reinforcing the organizational levers that influence innovation and looking more closely at those that seem to have no relationship or have a negative relationship with innovation. (See pp. 42–43.)

Are the lessons from this study applicable to new contract-related initiatives or to other Air Logistics Centers? We hypothesize that it is reasonable to think the dynamics between organizational levers and contract innovation at Warner Robins ALC are similar to the dynamics of these variables at both Oklahoma City and Ogden ALCs. However, it is also possible that, because this study analyzed contracts at a center viewed by HQ AFMC as particularly innovative, these results would not apply to the other two centers. Also, senior leadership at the other ALCs may have had a different impact on personnel behavior at their particular center. One would have to conduct a similar analysis at the other ALCs to know whether Warner Robins represents a unique case.

Could the same relationship between levers and innovation that we find under the CREP initiative occur with other contract initiatives? After all, the Air Force has taken on many other contracting-related initiatives since CREP. Many of those attempt more significant change in behaviors and even organizational structure, such as the purchasing and supply chain management (PSCM) initiative.[1] If senior leadership does not address those levers identified as having no relationship or having a negative relationship with innovation, then leadership may have to work as diligently—or more, depending on the initiative—to implement other innovative practices, much as it did for CREP. (See pp. 43–44.)

As senior leadership considers the behavioral implications of contracting initiatives such as CREP in the future, this study should provide suggestions as to what leadership needs to strengthen or understand better if it wants personnel to implement contract innova-

---

[1]The PSCM initiative, demonstrated on the F100 engine at Oklahoma City ALC in FY2002, has as its objective a strategic means of selecting and managing suppliers to provide more effective and efficient support to the warfighter. While consistent with CREP outcome goals, PSCM tries to do much more than CREP. PSCM would work with purchasing and supply chain activities from an enterprise- to operating-level perspective. It is strategic in scope and implies new processes, practices, and organizational structure. Behavioral implications for PSCM are more significant than CREP. See *Talking Paper on Adopting Improved Purchasing and Supply Chain Management*, Headquarters U.S. Air Force, Installations and Logistics, Supply Chain Integration and Logistics Transformation (HAF/IL-I), November 25, 2002. Also, see Nancy Y. Moore et al., *Implementing Purchasing and Supply Management Practices: Lessons from Innovative Commercial Firms*, RAND, DB-334-AF, 2002. Available at http://www.rand.org/publications/DB/DB334/.

tion. This study also provides an analytical approach to updating the relationship between organizational levers and new forms of contract innovation. Since this study began, the Air Force has added contract-related initiatives that are more complicated than CREP in their approach and expected outcomes—for example, PSCM, corporate contracting, and performance-based contracting. This study thus offers a methodology that can analyze the relationship between individual organizational levers and contract innovation. Organizational levers and their relationship with behavior and innovation continue to be of great interest to the Air Force, especially as it transforms to the changing threat environment and takes on ever more aggressive contract innovation and PSCM implementation efforts.

ACKNOWLEDGMENTS

The research described in this report was part of a larger effort led by Frank Camm and Nancy Moore that examined barriers to implementing acquisition reform initiatives for Air Force logistics contracting and sourcing. This study analyzed the relationship between the various ways senior leadership encouraged reform and innovation during the CREP initiative. This effort coincided with acquisition reform implementation in logistics contracts.

We were very grateful for the support Warner Robins ALC senior leadership, specifically, Stephen Davis (WR-ALC/CD) and George Falldine (WR-ALC/XP), gave to this effort. We appreciated the tremendous assistance that Jim Grant (WR-ALC/LKT, formerly PKP), provided us in helping set up many interviews with personnel considered by their peers as particularly innovative. We received significant support from Connie Black (WR-ALC/RE), who helped us understand how Warner Robins ALC was changing its processes under CREP and introduced us to CREP converters—those individuals responsible for leading the initiative within their respective product directorates.

Thanks to Mr. Davis' support, we had access to all product directorate chiefs for one-time interviews, to CREP converters, and to 177 personnel who participated on Contract Repair Teams and in our web-based CREP survey in 1998 and 1999. CREP converters helped us identify key members of the CRTs to include in the survey. Much of the anecdotal information that shaped both the contract design and behavioral models came from in-depth interviews with those CRTs. We thank those individuals whom we interviewed, those who helped us identify potential survey participants, and everyone who participated in the survey.

Jason Lingel and Eric Bird provided outstanding assistance in designing and coding the web-based, online survey. Eric provided the programming expertise for the survey in 1998. Jason created an automatic means of tailoring the survey to past individual responses in 1999, so that the follow-on survey incorporated prior responses and identified missing answers. In 1999, new participants received blank survey forms. Jason and Eric made it possible for us to conduct a completely paperless survey, which greatly facilitated our data analysis efforts and we hope made it easy for CRT members to complete.

Frank Camm and Laura Baldwin contributed significantly to this study. Frank Camm supported this study throughout by providing helpful feedback on its methodology, reviewing our findings, and commenting at length, which markedly enhanced the report. Laura Baldwin also provided many insightful, helpful comments. Megan Abbott, a communications analyst, helped us convey the information effectively to a general audience.

We are grateful for our two reviewers, Dr. Brett Katzman, Assistant Professor of Economics, School of Business Administration, University of Miami; and Dr. Marla Haims, Associate Scientist, RAND. Their careful reviews improved the final product and helped to clarify the message.

This effort required a great deal of data collection, scrubbing, synthesis, and modeling. Again, we are especially grateful for the comprehensive assistance Warner Robins ALC provided this study. The authors take responsibility for the analysis, content, and interpretations found in this report.

AFMC	Air Force Materiel Command
AL	Agile Logistics
ALC	Air Logistics Center
AR	Acquisition Reform
AREP	Aircraft Repair Enhancement Program
CREP	Contract Repair Enhancement Program
CRI	Consolidated Repairable Inventory
CRT	Contract Repair Team
CSI	Consolidated Serviceable Inventory
DLR	Depot Level Recoverable or Depot Level Repairable
DCAA	Defense Contract Audit Agency
DCMA	Defense Contract Management Agency
DREP	Depot Repair Enhancement Program
IMS	Item Management Specialist
IPT	Integrated Product Team
LRU	Line Replacement Unit
MICAP	Mission Capable
NIIN	National Item Identification Number
NSN	National Stock Number
PCA	Principal Components Analysis
PCO	Procurement Contracting Officer
PD	Product Directorate
PM/LO	Program Manager/Logistics Officer
PMS	Production Management Specialist
PSCM	Purchasing and Supply Chain Management
RBL	Readiness Based Leveling
SAF/AQC	Secretary of the Air Force, Deputy Assistant Secretary for Contracting

SOO	Statement of Objective
SOW	Statement of Work
SRU	Shop Replacement Unit
WR-ALC	Warner Robins Air Logistics Center

Chapter One

INTRODUCTION

The U.S. Air Force has tried for some years to reform business and contracting practices by attempting to implement best commercial practices in its logistics support services. Many of the ideas for improving the way it purchases these products and services come under the heading of acquisition reform (AR) or more recently, acquisition excellence, which falls under the Deputy Assistant Secretary of the Air Force (Contracting) (SAF/AQC). Acquisition reform showed that best practices could lead to dramatic cost improvements and accelerated program schedules in the acquisition of major weapon systems, such as aircraft and missiles. Soon after, the Air Force tried to apply similar best practices to depot-level services to deliver products and services that were "better, faster, and cheaper." Specifically, it wanted to bring improved savings and effectiveness to an area that has proven unusually difficult to shrink in size—depot-level maintenance and repair—while still meeting readiness goals. However, the pace of implementing its acquisition reform efforts occurred slowly. In response, the Air Force asked RAND for help in understanding what might be hindering personnel from implementing reform more quickly. If the right policies were in place but the pace of improvements in logistics support services was slower than desired, then a natural place to look for explanation is in those tools senior leadership use to foster specific personnel behavior and ultimately innovation. In the business world, these tools are frequently termed "organizational levers." Our study thus looked closely at the organizational levers in place during the Air Force's reform efforts and their relationship to repair contract innovation.

BACKGROUND

In 1995, the Air Force initiated efforts to improve logistics through its "lean logistics" model.[1] Lean logistics was meant to improve aircraft availability through faster repair cycle times for depot-level repairables (DLRs), prioritized repair, and faster transportation. Such improvements might also reduce the size and cost of supply inventories and thus reduce the in-place resources and assets necessary to support deployed forces, a signature goal of the efforts that followed and eventually incorporated lean logistics, today known as agile logistics. Agile logistics better captured the objective of "[restructuring] the worldwide logistics system to equip operational commanders and their combat forces with increased deployment speed, range and maneuverability."[2] Over the next year, the Air Force Materiel Command (AFMC) initiated the Depot Repair Enhancement Program (DREP) and Aircraft Repair Enhancement Program (AREP). DREP's attempts to enhance user-oriented metrics, such as "not mission-capable due to supply" and AWP (awaiting parts) time, and initial improvements seen in the performance of Air Force-owned, organic (noncontracted) repair activities made it obvious that aircraft availability objectives could not be met without also improving contract repair processes. In fact, the long contract-repair schedules for some units stymied efforts at reducing organic repair schedules for other units. As a companion to these programs, in 1995 AFMC developed the Contract Repair Enhancement Program (CREP) to mirror the agile logistics goals at the contract-repair level.

In 1996, independent of CREP, the Department of Defense (DoD) began AR efforts. Specifically, DoD extended AR goals and objectives that had been developed for the acquisition of large weapon systems to the purchasing of logistics support. In comparison with lean and agile logistics efforts, which were originally focused on improving *organic* rather than *contract* operations, AR paid more attention to specific contract design goals and processes used successfully by

---

[1]The PACER LEAN initiative launched in 1995 applied lean logistics concepts to selected systems at each Air Logistics Center (ALC). These prototypes were supposed to identify process changes needed to speed component repair.

[2]Lt Gen William P. Hallin, "Agile logistics: Where we've been, where we're going," *Air Force News*, April 28, 1998.

private-sector firms. AR emphasized greater contractor participation in specifying the repair process, the elimination of unnecessary data-reporting requirements, early involvement of the supplier in contract design formulation, and other practices used in the commercial world to reduce costs and enhance support.

Because of the similarity in goals between agile logistics and acquisition reform, acquisition reform tenets were added to CREP's already existing agile logistics tenets in 1996. CREP was thus designed to incorporate the best of both AR and lean logistics, adopting the faster repair cycle time emphasis of lean logistics and the better contract design and contract process objectives of acquisition reform.

When the data for this study were collected in 1998 and 1999, CREP operated under the assumption that major changes in how contracts were written should improve cycle time, cost, and quality. To encourage Contract Repair Teams (CRTs) to consider a wide spectrum of innovations that were consistent with acquisition reform and agile logistics goals, HQ AFMC developed a checklist of 16 CREP tenets that it wanted the ALCs to consider incorporating in their CREP contracts. These tenets were based on the Air Force's original acquisition reform initiatives and on lean logistics reforms (later called agile logistics reforms).

All CREP tenets on the checklist applied to at least one of the improvement areas mentioned above, i.e., improved cycle time, cost, and quality. For example, CREP called for functional expert teaming at the outset and early contractor involvement. This teaming was ultimately supposed to lead to better coordination between requirements and contract conditions, shorter administrative lead-time, and improved contracts, along with a reduction in overall costs. In addition, as part of its AR philosophy, CREP allowed the contractor more say in how repairs were accomplished. CREP also removed non-value-added and unnecessary government requirements in contracts to reduce contractor costs; in special cases, this reform may lead to more competition for governmental contracts and the entrance of new suppliers.[3] Many of the overarching objectives of

---

[3]Most repair contracts, measured in dollars, are sole source. (Sole sources of repair can arise if the contractor owns the technical data, which raises a barrier to new entrants, or if the market is limited, such as with obsolete technology or items with low

CREP were embodied in the use of innovative contract tenets that were reported to HQ AFMC by the CRTs. The tenets were a practical means of translating the strategic goals of "faster, better, cheaper" into tactical goals that could be measured and incorporated in contracts and the contracting process.

One goal of CREP—to speed repairs—has the potential benefit of cutting overall costs, provided the increased speed costs less than replenishing the inventory with new spares. AFMC developed a cost-benefit analysis tool to help personnel compare the cost of shortening repair cycle time with the cost of new inventory associated with the current repair cycle time.[4] In sum, a number of CREP innovations are meant to ensure the Air Force provides responsive service while improving the contract itself and streamlining the contract process.

Still, as noted earlier, reform has been slow. Thus, to identify the barriers to acquisition reform implementation, this study examined the incorporation of CREP tenets in repair contracts at an Air Force Air Logistics Center. The study tried to link this incorporation to various organizational levers, or policies and practices senior leadership has at its disposal to encourage and influence individual behavior, especially behavior at the operating level where most repair contracts are written.

At present, the Air Force conducts its logistics services at three AFMC ALCs: Oklahoma City in Oklahoma, Ogden in Utah, and Warner Robins in Georgia. These ALCs provide serviceable parts to their customers through the purchase of new parts and the repair of unserviceable or recoverable items. For our study, we chose to focus on acquisition reform and agile logistics implementation at Warner Robins ALC because its senior leadership had aggressively pursued

---

failure rates.) Thus, this change may have an effect, albeit a minor one. Primarily commercial systems, such as business jets used by senior leadership in the field, benefit the most from the removal of military specifications and standards. Removal of standards and specifications on combat-essential weapon systems must be done carefully; the benefit here primarily reduces costs to the sole-source provider.

[4]At the time of this study, only about 10 percent of CREP items were in a buy position, which meant that most items required cycle-time reductions at no additional cost. In some cases, CRTs accomplished this through reengineering the repair process, which required ALC approval.

CREP and gave it significant attention from the beginning of the initiative. Warner Robins also officially reported the second highest number of CREP contracts to HQ AFMC, providing a large number of observations from a single center.[5]

Between December 1996 and September 1998, each ALC evaluated its repair contracts for consistency with CREP goals.[6] The evaluation consisted of determining the number of CREP tenets incorporated using the 16-item checklist of tenets developed from the ALCs' initial experience in applying agile logistics and best practices to their first prototype CREP contracts. After the establishment of the checklist, HQ AFMC required the ALCs to report quarterly on the number of these tenets they had incorporated in DLR contracts, either through modifications or new contracts (more details about 16 goals are in Chapter Two of this report). Although the metric served as an administrative device to track the pace of acquisition reform in repair contracts, its criteria for classifying the inclusion of specific tenets in a contract were not clearly defined, as reported by interviewed Warner Robins ALC personnel.[7] CREP tenet reporting ended in September 1998. This metric was the best available formal Air Force summary measure on contracts the ALCs consider "improved" under the tenets incorporated on those contracts.

NEEDED BEHAVIORAL CHANGES

Improvements in the contract repair processes do not come without some tradeoffs to the Air Force. There are aspects of CREP that may make repair more costly initially or locally. On the other hand, these

---

[5]In September 1998, the five Air Force ALCs reported the following total number of contracts that had incorporated CREP tenets: Ogden ALC, 20; Oklahoma City ALC, 54; Sacramento ALC, 82; San Antonio ALC, 229; Warner Robins ALC, 101. San Antonio stands out because it appeared to report CREP tenets on contract modifications in addition to basic contract numbers, unlike the other four ALCs. If one were restricted to contract numbers alone, San Antonio's number would have dropped from 229 to 152. Viewed this way, Warner Robins looked like a good place to study CREP contracts.

[6]*Contract Repair Enhancement Program (CREP) Phase III Implementation: A Briefing,* Warner Robins ALC, February 19 , 1997.

[7]As an example, one CREP tenet is to reduce military standards and specifications. It is unclear whether the reduction of one standard or specification was enough for a CRT to report success in using this tenet.

initiatives may ultimately reduce long-term total costs. For example, CREP requires that the contractor assume some risk in terms of equipment and manpower availability—so that they may perform efficient repair work on short notice (i.e., "just-in-time" repair on demand). In turn, for work in which there is only one contractor working on items that require expensive repair, CRTs considered allowing contractors to order long-lead-time material at Air Force expense (i.e., allowing the contractor to lay in parts needed for the repair before the repair actually occurred). These concepts are not new, but their use on certain repair contracts appears to have expanded. Additionally, working toward shorter repair cycle times involves a tradeoff. Contractors may be able to provide a product more quickly—the stated goal of agile logistics—but it may come with increased unit repair cost to the Air Force. These innovations, however, are still preferable when they lead to overall reduced total ownership costs.

Implicit in some CREP tenets, such as early contractor involvement, is a change in how and when the contractor is brought into the contracting process. Laying in long-lead-time material, for instance, required senior leadership approval and also implied changes to the process. For teams to achieve the incorporation of some tenets, teams had to go beyond traditional methods and had to build business cases to meet requirements in new ways that were consistent with CREP. These differences in solving contracting problems were not specifically recorded but were implicit in many of the CREP tenets. The challenge to senior leadership was to encourage individuals to take the new practices and policies provided by acquisition reform and agile logistics and implement innovation, even though methods for achieving innovation—the incorporation of CREP tenets—had to be discovered, learned, and refined. The implementation of CREP required CRTs to behave differently. Senior leadership had instructed CRTs to implement CREP and had various tools to encourage changed behavior from CRT team members, which we turn to next.

This study took the approach that senior leadership has available organizational levers or methods by which it can influence individual behavior at the operational level for contracting. It did not address process changes brought about by this initiative. AFMC adopted the Integrated Product Team (IPT) approach of CREP with its Contract

Repair Teams, along with the early acquisition reform and agile logistics goals and approaches as standard practice.[8] Some of the most important process changes, such as the use of the cost-benefit analysis tool and teaming, were available to all CRTs at the same time. Our study focused on differences in CREP tenet incorporation outcomes with respect to teams and organizational levers. We were particularly interested in what influenced depot-level personnel to implement CREP and what leadership could do to further encourage innovation implementation.[9]

This report considers how organizational levers are associated with change in contract design and the contract process through their relationship with personnel attitudes and behaviors. For any major change in business practice to succeed over the long run, preferred behavior must not be a temporary shift or allowed to revert to the old ways once senior leadership attention moves on to another initiative.

In a separate analysis we conducted on contracts written during the CREP initiative, we found that contracts incorporating CREP tenets had different outcomes than non-CREP contracts. Data on recoverable items on CREP and non-CREP contracts written over a similar period showed statistically unchanged repair prices for CREP items compared with non-CREP items. On average, prices increased for non-CREP items, but they held steady for CREP components. Negotiated flow days—the repair cycle time required by the contract—for items on CREP and non-CREP contracts showed real improvements, i.e., they were both less than their respective previous contract flow days. Although the flow days for non-CREP items improved more than for CREP items, i.e., they decreased from previous flow days,

---

[8]Before CREP, ALC personnel processed the requirements, writing and negotiating the contract in a series of sequential steps. Personnel formally assembled jointly at the end of this process at a Contract Management Review Board (CMRB) meeting. With CREP, personnel met as a Contract Repair Team at the beginning of the process to make decisions collectively. This procedure allowed teams to make major changes in contracts that otherwise might not have occurred because of the approval needed by all functional experts.

[9]Factors other than organizational levers may have accounted for the incorporation of CREP tenets. Technically, these other factors are captured in the regression residual variables. Recognizing that factors other than organizational levers can explain reform, we examined unit price and repair flow day differences in CREP and non-CREP contracts written about the same time (see Appendix A). The comparison captures the effect of all factors influencing CRT behavior during the study period.

they did so with higher prices. Flow days for CREP items decreased at the same time their prices remained essentially unchanged. Appendix A discusses these results.

Even though the introductory phase of the reform process is over, opportunities for repair contract improvements continue.[10] As contracts written early in the initiative expire, CRTs have a chance to apply the lessons learned to date to write even better contracts. In addition, as best practices evolve and private-sector firms continuously improve costs, product quality, and schedule, CRTs can benefit from these greater efficiencies as successive generations of CREP contracts expire.

As senior leadership attention moves on to new problems and issues, the continued pace of reform implementation will depend on the extent to which the Air Force leadership and the organization can encourage new, desired behavior. This study's findings suggest two types of lessons from CREP. First, our results suggest that at Warner Robins ALC, many of the senior leadership's organizational levers had a positive relationship with contract innovation. These levers are a sign of success and suggest that those policies and practices AFMC and Warner Robins ALC used for CREP were constructive. Second, there are indications that other organizational levers were not related to innovation. These levers need to be investigated; if they are not understood and addressed, they could continue to have a negative or neutral relationship to contract innovation.

Having thus outlined the CREP initiative that served as the focus of our study, let us now turn to the next chapter, which describes this study's approach and, in particular, the survey conducted at Warner Robins ALC to measure organizational levers. Chapter Three presents the results of the regression analyses we conducted on the survey data with respect to tenet use and discusses the significance and implications for the implementation of acquisition reform and other Air Force initiatives. A series of appendices provides detailed discussions on technical topics. Appendix A shows several histograms describing changes in price and schedule for items in CREP and non-

---

[10]Even though the Air Force has changed its contract repair process along the lines of the CREP initiative, CREP has been a clearinghouse for contract reform and contract process changes.

CREP contracts. Appendix B provides a copy of the questions used to structure interviews conducted in April 1998 and June 1998 with CRTs. Appendix C provides a copy of the web-based survey as it appeared to participants. Appendix D discusses the principal components analyses conducted on the survey data used to create the independent variables—organizational levers—in the regression analyses. Finally, Appendix E provides the detailed results of the regression analyses.

Chapter Two

METHODOLOGICAL APPROACH

Senior leadership can play a vital role in affecting change in business practices through its capacity to set new goals and objectives, communicate them throughout all levels of the organization, and modify performance evaluation and incentives in ways that encourage personnel to adopt those new business practices. Success at the operating level depends on how effectively senior leadership can move personnel toward changed behavior and maintain that behavior long after an initiative becomes standard operating policy. The tools leadership has to motivate line-operator personnel are what this study refers to as "organizational levers," i.e., those means by which leadership encourages and influences individual behavior to achieve certain policy goals and objectives.

This chapter describes our study methodology; in particular, we describe our process of measuring the organizational levers in use at Warner Robins ALC—levers designed to stimulate the use of CREP tenets in repair contracts. We then outline the survey we conducted at Warner Robins ALC to assess behaviors and attitudes toward acquisition reform. Specifically, the survey measured organizational levers at Warner Robins ALC during the CREP initiative. This chapter also describes the regression models we developed to explore the relationship between these levers and number of select CREP tenets incorporated in a contract.

Achieving improvements in ALC contract repair outcomes is complex. The large variety of contracts and the number of contractors with whom ALCs work mean operating-level personnel must have significant motivation to translate senior leadership policy guidance and directives into each repair contract. Improved repair outcomes from contractors do not happen by Air Force fiat, particularly because personnel at contract repair facilities answer to their own corporate leadership, not to the Air Force. Thus, to generate better outcomes, Air Force senior leadership faces challenges to find ways to motivate its contract repair teams to write the kinds of contracts that ultimately lead to improved performance from contractors and to manage the Air Force-contractor relationship from a mutually beneficial perspective.

How does the Air Force seek to galvanize its contract repair teams so that they write innovative contracts and manage the Air Force-contractor relationship more effectively and consistently? Senior leadership generally uses a series of levers that influence specific kinds of organizational practices and behavior. If these organizational levers are aligned and operating as Air Force senior leadership intends, one would expect to see the kind of relationship between levers and contract outcomes the Air Force wants—i.e., organizational levers help explain contract measures of success with respect to the contract initiative, such as CREP.

To examine Warner Robins ALC's use of organizational levers and the outcome on contract innovation, this study followed three steps. First, we conducted a *literature review and interviews* with key personnel at an ALC. Second, we developed a *survey* based on the review and interviews and administered it to personnel on CREP Contract Repair Teams. Third, we conducted a series of *analyses* that ultimately established through empirical means a relationship between organizational levers and a contract measure of innovation— that is, the number of CREP tenets incorporated in repair contracts. The analyses involved a three-part process. One phase of the analytical process used principal components analysis (PCA) on the survey responses to identify questions associated with specific organizational levers (the independent variables). Another phase of the analytical process developed five groups of specific kinds of CREP tenets incorporated in repair contracts (the dependent variables). The final phase of the analytical process involved *regression analyses* to determine whether organizational levers could help explain the extent to which these grouped tenets were incorporated in repair contracts. These CREP tenets were considered by AFMC as improvements to be implemented in logistics support contracts and measures of innovation. The reader can refer to Appendix B for the interview questions and Appendix C for the PCA technique used to determine the organizational levers. Each of these steps is described in more detail below.

LITERATURE REVIEW AND INTERVIEWS

The Air Force's shift to acquisition reform and new business practices mirrors private-sector transformation efforts in that it requires significant changes in organizational behaviors and attitudes. The study team reviewed the literature on organizational transformation to identify those elements considered key in helping commercial firms transform their business practices and organizations. The review indicated that companies that have successfully pursued large-scale transformation have made changes to all of their major organizational subsystems, including work structures and processes, training and rewards systems, and organizational culture. The CREP initiative attempted smaller-scale changes that focused on encouraging new behaviors from the organization using new policies and slightly different processes, such as teaming, cost-benefit analyses, and early contractor involvement.

Literature Review

The literature on successful organizational change within private-sector firms argues that a key element to instituting such transformation is leadership support (Strebel, 1996; Katzenbach and Smith, 1993; Larkin and Larkin, 1994). All levels of management must openly promote a consistent platform of change in order to motivate employee working modes.

Typically, employees resist change in work behavior unless incentives are in place to reward new behaviors. The literature suggests necessary steps for incentives to change behavior successfully. First, management must provide clear standards of evaluation that are aligned with performance goals (Pfeffer, 1996; Strebel, 1996). Next, Pfeffer (1996) and Strebel (1996) suggest that leaders must provide feedback on whether employee performance is leading to better contract performance. Finally, consistent rewards and/or sanctions are needed to reinforce behavior over time (Ghoshal and Bartlett,

1996).   The effectiveness of rewards will be realized only if con-tracting personnel are told how to achieve them (Pfeffer, 1996).

To ensure that new contracting practices continue to be imple-mented over time, psychological barriers of change must also be ad-dressed.   Part of leadership's responsibility is to instill the under-standing that implementing new contracting practices will lead to improved contract performance.   Employees need "proof" that these new methods will help them create a better contract (Larkin and Larkin, 1994). Addressing these needs can facilitate the continuation of changed behaviors and attitudes past the introductory phase.

In sum, the literature on successful organizational transformation suggests that permanent changes in contracting personnel behavior will come only through consistent, thorough support by Air Force leadership.   This support may be demonstrated in a number of ways: consistent communication of support by leadership, incentives for new behaviors, training and skill development, and performance feedback.   These factors should lead to changes in employee atti-tudes that then promote innovation.   Changes in attitudes will help maintain new behaviors over time.

A review of the literature identified at the highest, general level the kinds of organizational levers that private-sector firms have found to be important in their own transformational efforts.   The levers from the review became topics for discussion in interviews with Warner Robins ALC personnel who were selected by the ALC as innovative in writing CREP contracts.   Interviews at Warner Robins ALC then helped the study team construct a survey that would eventually be used to measure organizational levers.   We next describe the inter-views.

Interviews

The interviews conducted at Warner Robins ALC provided the study team insight on how organizational levers operated at the center during the CREP initiative.   We were interested in listening to the language that CRT personnel used when talking about these levers and the issues raised.   These interviews influenced the way we framed our survey questions.

The study team conducted three sets of meetings at Warner Robins ALC to accomplish three objectives. During the first set of meetings (March 10–11, 1998), we met with all key CREP stakeholders to communicate our study's goals and objectives and to gain product directorate leadership approval to interview their personnel. We first met with personnel at Warner Robins ALC who could help us gain support of the product directorate chiefs to conduct a survey of their personnel. In particular, we met with the chiefs of Plans and Programs (XP), Contracts (PK), and Reengineering (RE). (Warner Robins ALC/RE was a facilitating office for processes and practices needed to implement CREP.) We also met with chiefs and/or their staff in the then-product directorates of Ground Equipment (LB), C-5 (LC), F-15 (LF), Electronic Warfare (LN), U-2 (LR), Special Operations Forces (LU), and Avionics (LY). In these meetings, we conveyed the study's goals and established contact with those CRTs considered by Warner Robins ALC/PK and Warner Robins ALC/RE as especially innovative in their CREP implementation. These high-level meetings were critical in helping us to gain access to individuals with whom we conducted in-depth interviews and ultimately surveyed.

Most of the full-scale interview data were collected during the second and third sets of meetings at Warner Robins ALC. In the second set of meetings (April 7–8, 1998), we met with CRT members in LF, LR, LN, LK, LU, and LY. In the third set of meetings (June 8–9, 1988), we met with CRT members in LN and LU. The meetings took place in groups to minimize ALC time and effort. We interviewed program managers, procurement contracting officers, production management specialists, and item management specialists. Participants were given a list of questions before the meeting. (Appendix B presents the interview questions.) We asked interviewees to think about the questions within the context of a specific contract the center considered most innovative or successful in incorporating CREP tenets.

We then asked a series of questions about the contracts they had in mind, covering such areas as:

- *Background of the contract:* general description and characteristics

- *Contracting process:* differences in the process as a result of CREP

- *CRT/IPT:* how teams were created, who participated, how the teams worked together
- *Design of the contract:* innovations considered and incorporated; challenges and methods of resolution
- *Lessons learned:* what the CRT learned, what individual team members learned, how lessons were transmitted to other teams.

Individuals discussed their experiences with particular CREP contracts. Using the context of a specific contract, we asked questions or guided discussions toward topics related to organizational levers. Individuals told us what worked and what was most difficult in incorporating CREP tenets. The information from these interviews, along with the organizational levers identified in the literature review, was used to develop the survey questions.

We next discuss the survey conducted at Warner Robins ALC. The survey asked members of CRTs how strongly they agreed with a series of statements about acquisition reform, leadership, performance evaluation and rewards, teaming and partnering, and training and career development. (The survey questions are reproduced in Appendix C.)

SURVEY OF WARNER ROBINS ALC

Data were collected on organizational levers through a survey of key members of contract repair teams. To develop the survey, we relied on the aforementioned literature review findings and on in-depth interviews conducted with CRTs identified by Warner Robins ALC as on the cutting edge of writing innovative contracts. The survey included those elements considered in the literature as important in eliciting new behaviors from individuals in private-sector organizations. For the survey, we adapted these elements to a CREP context and emphasized issues considered as key drivers or inhibitors of innovation by the individuals interviewed at the ALC. Warner Robins ALC senior leadership reviewed the survey questions; we also ran a pilot test with a few people who worked on CRTs to identify potential wording or interpretation problems. (The survey questions are in Appendix C.)

Conducted over two periods—in 1998 and 1999—the web-based survey asked questions on perceptions of acquisition reform and its implementation as well as questions concerning individual behavior and incentives. The survey was distributed to four positions in each CRT that the teams themselves considered the most significant in the design and writing of contracts—the program manager or logistics officer (PM/LO), the item management specialist (IMS), the procurement contracting officer (PCO), and the production management specialist-seller (PMS). Each person who participated provided only one set of responses.

These four CRT member positions play critical roles in the contract process. The program manager, for instance, heads the CRT and is responsible for managing weapon systems assets. The IMS is responsible for estimating requirements, such as the number of repairs for a particular group of items over a time horizon. Repair production-related issues during contract execution fall to the PMS, who works from the ALC side to anticipate and resolve issues that arise during repair actions.[1] PCOs understand contracting policy and regulations and actually write the contract. They prepare documentation to support contract review, write the contract, negotiate the terms and conditions, translate various decisions and agreements into legally binding language, and help select the contractors.

Overall, the response rate for the survey was 64 percent.[2] Although the survey went to four positions per contract team, many of the individuals in those positions sat on more than one CRT and were associated with more than one contract. This phenomenon had the effect of smoothing out some of the variation in the independent variables, because the responses of an individual could apply to more than one contract. In 1998, we received responses from CRTs

---

[1] During CREP, if ALC-owned and operated organic shops also conducted some of the repair workload, two PMSs participated: the buyer PMS, who worked with the IMS to establish the requirement for contract repair, and the seller PMS, who worked with the PCO to construct a contract. Because it focused on CREP, this study's survey involved only seller PMSs.

[2] The sample consisted of 256 individuals: 66 PCOs, 40 PMSs, 75 PMs, and 75 IMSs. A breakdown by position revealed a 74 percent response rate from PCOs (n = 49), a 63 percent response rate from PMSs (n = 25), a 60 percent response rate from PMs (n = 45) and a 60 percent response rate from IMSs (n = 45). Data were analyzed from 79 unique CRTs that wrote 101 contracts.

responsible for 84 contracts written primarily in 1997 and 1998. In 1999, we again surveyed some of the CRT members whose first responses contained missing data. Other members who had not responded at all were again asked to participate. By asking CRT members to complete their surveys or participate if they had not responded in the first survey, the number of contracts in our sample increased from 84 to 101. Expanding the sample size to 101 contracts or observations increased the likelihood the regression analyses would detect significance in levers related to tenet implementation. The number of contracts in our sample was an important constraint in the analyses, because it limited the number of independent variables used in the regression analyses.[3]

ORGANIZATIONAL LEVERS (INDEPENDENT VARIABLES) IDENTIFIED PRIMARILY THROUGH PRINCIPAL COMPONENTS ANALYSES

We analyzed survey responses using a technique called Principal Components Analysis that allows one to examine relationships among item responses to determine whether particular questions reflect the same underlying concept. It is a general method of developing scales in the social sciences, used for example in personality and intelligence scales.[4] Specifically, the PCA technique enabled us to construct eight organizational lever variables from responses to survey questions that were closely aligned and addressed a common theme. We first describe PCA and the eight independent variables that emerged from that process. Next we describe two independent variables that were computed directly. At the end of this section, we discuss the final steps in constructing the independent variables. Appendix C shows the original survey, and the next section discusses those questions that made up the independent variables.

---

[3]We would have liked to include additional variables in the regression models to help control for potential systematic bias in the survey responses, e.g., dummy variables for job title of respondents, etc.; unfortunately, the small size of our sample limited the addition of such variables.

[4]See B. G. Tabachnick and L. S. Fidell, *Using Multivariate Statistics*, Third Edition, New York: Harper Collins, 1996.

PCA showed that the survey questions consisted of eight separate themes describing organizational levers. These levers were named: attitude toward acquisition reform, leadership consistency, performance evaluation, performance incentives, effective teaming, contractor partnering, Air Force partnering, and training in acquisition reform. Details of the PCA can be found in Appendix D. Additionally, the survey questions used to construct each organizational lever variable are provided at the end of each variable's description below.

Attitude Toward Acquisition Reform

During the early part of the acquisition reform initiative in 1996 and 1997, contracting personnel throughout the Department of Defense communicated a belief that reform was generally a good idea, but perhaps not for operating-line personnel, particularly if better contracts meant the individual's workload would increase and fewer people would be needed to do the work in the future. Some people perceived that contract outcome improvements might jeopardize their jobs. Still others saw benefits in solving certain problems to free up their time to solve harder problems.

The PCA technique identified two related survey questions that asked about support for acquisition reform. The first question asked about the extent to which the person supported the goals of acquisition reform. The second question, with five subparts, asked about the person's perception of how acquisition reform would affect his or her contracts and job. The questions were:

- How supportive are you of the goals of acquisition reform? (Q25)

- How likely is acquisition reform to contribute to the following outcomes? (Q26)

  - Improve mission capability rates for end user

  - Reduce the cost of my contracts

  - Increase contractor responsiveness/flexibility

  - Increase my job satisfaction

  - Make my job more secure.

Responses to these questions formulated the attitude organizational lever variable.

Leadership Consistency

AFMC and the ALCs are under tremendous pressure to apply best practices where it makes sense, and consequently they have a large number of initiatives underway. It is natural for operating-level personnel to work more aggressively on an initiative to which they believe their immediate supervisor and senior leadership appear committed and that they expect will lead to permanent change. One would expect that the more people feel leadership is consistently calling them to enact reform, the more likely they will do so.

Principal components analysis indicated that two parts of a question on leadership support were related. These items measured the extent to which the person felt he or she was hearing the same message about reform from all levels of management and whether management appeared committed to reform over the long run. The questions were:

- How true are the following statements about acquisition reform? (Q28)
  - Different parts of the chain of command send different messages about AR.
  - Management attitudes suggest that AR is the latest "program of the month."

Performance Evaluation

The business and management science literature suggested that individuals perform best in areas in which they are evaluated and given incentives. Thus, if the success of acquisition reform depends on better teaming, improved contract performance, and better contractor relationships, then it follows that performance evaluation criteria for these areas are important. The more people feel they will be evaluated on reform success, the more likely they will try to implement reform innovation. This organizational lever must be viewed carefully, because the CREP initiative was still ongoing when it was measured. In interviews, we were told personnel evaluation criteria had not changed during the initiative, so we expected this variable to be weakly related to behavior for the contracts in our sample, if at all. Still, we included it, because of its importance in the literature.

PCA indicated four subparts of a question about performance evaluations were related:

- How important are the following factors in your yearly performance evaluation? (Q29)

  - Improving the timeliness of contracts processed (reduced administrative lead-time)

  - Working effectively with the members of my CRT

  - Improving contract performance (cost, reliability, cycle times)

  - Improving partnering with contractors.

Performance Incentives

Unlike performance evaluation criteria that already exist before the initiative, performance incentives often develop during an initiative, as happened at Warner Robins ALC. We identified performance rewards used by the private sector in a review of the business literature and those used by Warner Robins ALC in interviews with CRTs. Anecdotal evidence suggested center personnel used formal recognition from the organization (e.g., plaques) as a primary incentive for good performance. Several individuals we interviewed early in the study indicated positive feedback from customers (customer surveys, letters from customers) provided an effective incentive for them to continue to perform well, but others we interviewed thought voluntary customer recognition (letters or phone calls from customers) was too subjective and arbitrary. Some of the individuals we interviewed expressed concern that their hard work was not appreciated by customers or their immediate supervisors and, as a consequence, believed this lack of appreciation undermined their enthusiasm for taking on new challenges with new contracts. We expected to see more innovation as people perceived they would be rewarded for their success.

PCA found a relationship between items in a five-part survey question on performance incentives:

- How likely is the effective use of AR to lead to the following rewards? (Q30)
- Higher merit increases
- Improved opportunities for promotion
- Non-monetary rewards (e.g., time off, trips)
- Recognition from ALC/product directorate/division of a job well done
- Official acknowledgment of customer satisfaction.

Effective Teaming

As mentioned earlier, CREP emphasized the concept of bringing all key members together early in the contracting process to decide collectively on contract goals and strategy. This teaming concept allowed a better "give and take" with functional experts who, in the past, had not necessarily understood all of the practical and legal constraints by which other members were bound. CRTs also reported to us in interviews an appreciation for involving the contractor early in the process. In some cases, CRTs were able to change the contract fundamentally only after reviewing the contract repair process with the contractor, sharing information on projected requirements and learning from the contractor about particular problems in the contract repair facility to arrive at fundamental changes in the contract together. Effective teaming, however, meant that the team needed to overcome functional barriers, such as understanding primary objectives and constraints in each step of the process. As the team formulated a common strategy, team members had to agree to work toward a common performance goal and include early on anyone who had potential veto power over the proposed contract. We expected the relationship between effective teaming and innovation to be positive, i.e., as effective teaming increased, CRTs would be more innovative.

The PCA suggested these three teaming items were related:

- How true are the following statements about the CRTs (or IPTs) you have worked on? (Q32)

  - The CRT was effective in overcoming functional or disciplinary barriers to cooperation.

  - Team members worked toward a common performance goal.

  - Non-core CRT members (FM, BC, CR, EN, QA) were well integrated into the process.

Contractor Partnering

Most CRTs reported good relationships with their contractors and most had worked with those contractors for years. CREP set as its objective improvements in repair contract outcomes, which necessitated changing expectations (better performance) in repair contracts and in ways of working with contractors. We expected that innovation would occur more frequently with contractors perceived by team members to be contributing positively to the business relationship.[5]

The PCA technique found that four subquestions about contractor partnering were related:

- How true are the following statements about the relationship between the Air Force and the contractor? (Q34)

  - A positive working relationship exists with the contractor.

  - The Air Force and contractor have worked together to improve processes and reduce cycle time.

  - The contractor alerts the Air Force to anticipated problems that could affect the contractor's performance.

  - The contractor shows a willingness to assume risks in order to do business with the Air Force.

---

[5]Innovation can certainly occur under adversarial conditions, such as with the acquisition of new systems where the Air Force can dictate the terms unilaterally when there is competition. It is less likely to occur in an adversarial relationship with a sole-source supplier. Most of Air Force repair contracts are with sole-source suppliers.

Air Force Partnering

During interviews it appeared that PMs and PCOs were particularly concerned about the Air Force's ability to be a better customer to its suppliers. In particular, they were concerned about its willingness both to pay for the risk it expected the contractor to assume and to reward contractors who perform well. The prevailing approach in repair contracts over the years has been to put most of the risk on the contractor in the belief that it would minimize costs, because the Air Force would not pay for any workload that did not generate. Under acquisition reform and lean logistics, teams found they had to assume some risk up front to get the decreases in the repair prices and repair cycle times they wanted. Thus, we expected that as Air Force partnering increased or improved—measured as explicit treatment of risk and rewards—more innovation would occur.

PCA indicated two subquestions were related in regard to Air Force partnering:

- How true are the following statements about the relationship between the Air Force and the contractor? (Q34)

    - The Air Force shows a willingness to pay for the risks it wants the contractor to assume.

    - The Air Force shows a commitment to reward contractors who perform well.

Training in Acquisition Reform

The literature explicitly emphasizes the importance of training employees in how to integrate new practices into their jobs. Because the survey covered several topics and had resource constraints, it asked high-level questions only. For example, it measured quantity of training days but not the quality of the training received. In this study, we expected that as the number of days of training and frequency of updates people received increased, innovation would also increase.

Using results from the PCA technique, two survey questions were used to construct the "training in acquisition reform" variable. The first question asked how many days of formal training in acquisition reform a person received in the past two years. The second asked how often they received updates in acquisition reform training. These questions were:

- How many days of formal training in acquisition reform have you received in the past two fiscal years? (Q41)

- How often do you receive formal and informal training updates on acquisition reform as it affects your job? (Q42)

Two other independent variables were computed directly. The ninth organizational lever variable—years of job experience—used data collected in the survey but did not require PCA. The tenth variable— a product directorate dummy variable—also did not require PCA. We describe them next.

Job Experience

Work experience can have a positive and negative relationship to innovation. Long experience in a position can make a person better informed on past efforts that worked or failed. Such information can make someone either risk averse or more likely to succeed by knowing the potential pitfalls. Lack of experience, in turn, can make a person more willing to try something new and challenging. Anecdotal evidence from interviews with CRT personnel suggested that younger members were more enthusiastic and willing to write more innovative contracts. Therefore, we expected those with less job experience would be more likely to write innovative contracts.

We used one survey question to construct the "job experience" variable:

- How many years of work experience do you have in your current job? (Q35–38)

Product Directorate

At the time of this study, the U-2 Product Directorate at Warner Robins used large sustainment contracts to support its classified weapon systems instead of component repair contracts used by the unclassified programs. These sustainment contracts covered a variety of goods and services, including repair, modifications, engineering, new parts procurements, and scheduled overhauls. Because of classification requirements, they used separate data systems and slightly different contracting rules than did the CRTs in the other product directorates. Funds on U-2 contracts generally came from appropriated weapon system-specific funds that did not compete with parts from other weapon systems, as do items that use revolving fund dollars. For all of these reasons, we expected that the U-2 Product Directorate had more opportunities to innovate than did the other product directorates.

We tried to control for these differences in contracts with a dummy variable, called "Product Directorate," analogous to a commercial corporate division. If the CREP contract was written in the U-2 Product Directorate, we assigned the variable a value of 1; otherwise it received a 0.

This section described how PCA was used to identify organizational lever themes among the survey responses for eight independent variables and how two other variables were computed. We next discuss how the independent variables were computed for each organizational lever after the PCA analyses.

Independent Variable Computation

PCA indicated themes among survey questions that ultimately formed eight organizational variables. For each theme identified by PCA, such as leadership consistency, a respondent's values were summed across all of the questions considered by PCA as related.[6] The organizational lever variable for each contract was determined by averaging the values of individual team members across the CRT.

Because each member provided survey responses only once, responses sometimes resulted in duplicates if an individual participated in more than one CRT or contract. In most cases, CRTs consisted of a different set of members, thus making the indepen-

---

[6]Responses to survey questions took on values that ranged from 1 to 5 (or 1 to 3, in some cases) with a 1 assigned consistently to the lowest end of the scale. Thus, responses to survey questions associated with particular organizational lever variables were given a quantitative value.

dent variables not identical. Ideally, one would like to survey CRT members at the conclusion of each contract activity, but this study was allowed to conduct the survey once (the second survey collected responses from CRT members who had not responded during the first year of data collection or to complete missing data from the first survey). The survey responses represented an accumulated experience for CRT members. Response rates for CRT teams varied across contracts. The sample included contracts that had survey responses from at least one person on the CRT. Most of the sample contracts included responses from two or more CRT members.

We also evaluated the independent variables for the degree to which they were normally distributed, as required for ordinary least squares (OLS) regression analysis.[7] As a result, we transformed two variables—attitude toward acquisition reform and leadership consistency—from a 1 to 5 scale to a 1 to 3 scale because of the lack of variability across the 5-point scale. Leadership consistency and effective teaming were positively skewed, but a square root transformation led to a negatively skewed distribution, so we did not transform these variables. Distributions across the rest of the independent variables were not highly skewed.

CREP TENET GROUPS (DEPENDENT VARIABLES)

Now we turn to the identification of our dependent variables. For our analysis, the dependent variables were specific groups of tenets derived from CREP policy objectives. The CREP initiative had two primary policy objectives: contract innovations consistent with acquisition reform and innovations consistent with agile logistics. The study team developed dependent variables that policymakers could interpret strategically. Our study sponsor was interested in explaining strategic, policy-level outcomes, not tactical outcomes such as the implementation of individual tenets. Once we decided to use groups of CREP tenets as dependent variables, we then faced the issue of how to develop the groups. We initially conducted a cluster analysis of the CREP tenets in our sample of 101 contracts to identify empirically groups of CREP tenets. The cluster analysis identified

---

[7]We tested the need for transforming variables with the PROC UNIVARIATE function in SAS system software.

tenet groups that had no meaningful policy-relevant theme, which made these groupings unusable. In the end, we decided to formulate tenet groups based on policy themes highlighted in the CREP initiative itself and in a policy emphasized at the beginning of the initiative.[8] We next consider these policy themes in more detail.

CREP Tenets: Elements of the Dependent Variable

As noted earlier, during CREP implementation, HQ AFMC provided its ALCs with a 16-item checklist to use when considering tenets to incorporate in each CREP repair contract. For our regression analysis, we used these 16 CREP tenets in formulating our dependent variables. HQ AFMC monitored the use of this checklist, and each ALC reported the actual number of tenets incorporated in contracts on a quarterly basis. This information was the data source for the dependent variables for most of the contracts in our sample; that is, these reports became the basis for our determination of the extent of tenet incorporation. Eight contracts in the sample were written after September 1998, and thus the reporting of their tenet incorporation came directly from Warner Robins ALC.

The CREP tenets used in the analyses are listed and defined below.[9] The tenets involve acquisition reform and agile logistics-related concepts. When necessary, we provide definitions commonly accepted by the logistics community.

- *Reduce contract repair prices:* lower repair prices from those of the same item in the previous contract.

- *Reduce repair cycle time:* shorten repair cycle time—the time an item arrives at the contractor repair facility to when it leaves— from that in the previous contract.

---

[8]At the beginning of the CREP initiative, Warner Robins ALC tried to implement as many CREP tenets as possible in all candidate CREP contracts, which meant only the easiest tenets could be incorporated in still-active contracts. These easy-to-incorporate tenets were related to fast transportation and did not affect any of the other parts of the contract. These tenets are included in the "simple modifications" tenet group.

[9]CREP tenet heading language came from Warner Robins ALC, circa 1998.

- *Reduce administrative process days:* shorten administrative lead-time or the time it takes to write a contract from the very beginning.

- *Reduce inventories:* anticipated decrease in new spare buy requirements that result from a shorter repair cycle time or reductions in other parts of the repair pipeline, such as fast transportation.

- *Repair on demand:* repair demand set by the EXPRESS system, which tries to maximize the probability that all Air Force bases meet their aircraft availability goals through its computed repair priorities that depend on demand forecasts across a planning horizon, actual asset positions, and a host of logistics considerations.

- *Establish a consolidated repairable inventory/consolidated serviceable inventory (CRI/CSI):* the depot stock level, as computed by Readiness-Based Leveling (RBL) or some other method, which puts the pool of centrally held serviceable and unserviceable assets at the contractor facility rather than the managing ALC.

- *Direct shipment:* recoverable items sent directly from an Air Force base to a contractor and sent back to an Air Force base without passing through a Defense Logistics Agency serviceable warehouse at the managing ALC.

- *Maximize use of commercial practices:* practices used by private-sector firms with their commercial customers.

- *Performance-oriented specifications:* use of a statement of objective or a generalized set of performance goals, rather than a detailed set of work instructions that are specified by the Air Force.

- *Fast transportation:* use of expedited air transportation, as needed.

- *Shipment on demand:* shipment instructions for the newly produced serviceable that the Air Force transmits electronically to the contractor.

- *Early contractor involvement:* mainly used with sole-source contractors, although CRTs occasionally used face-to-face meetings with prospective bidders for competitive contracts. The CRT met with the contractor early in the process and involved the supplier in constructing the new contract, developing the statement of objective, and so forth.

- *Long-duration contract:* long-term contracts, defined by AFMC as three years or more.

- *Reduce military specifications and standards:* technical requirements eliminated without increased risk to the Air Force, potentially allowing contractors to use commercial specifications and standards and reduce contractor costs.

- *Eliminate unnecessary data requirements:* reporting requirements deemed outdated, duplicative, or underutilized could be eliminated, thus potentially reducing contractor costs and repair prices.

- *Contract performance incentives:* use of a clause that rewards or penalizes performance that deviates significantly from baseline expectations.

Figure 2.1 indicates the percentage of contracts that report using each innovation. More than half the contracts in the sample included 10 of the 16 CREP tenets, with most claiming long-duration contracts. The tenets used with the least frequency in the sample of contracts were contract performance incentives, shipment on demand, and reduced inventories. [10] Twenty-six percent of the sample contracts came from the U-2 Product Directorate, which we discuss at the end of the next section on the construction of the model's dependent variables.

---

[10] Anecdotal evidence from interviews suggests several reasons for the infrequent incorporation of these tenets. Performance incentives work well with objective methods of measuring performance and understanding the value of different performance criteria, e.g., the worth of getting an item returned in the five days versus ten days. Shipment on demand occurs routinely now, but at the time of the study data system changes were not available to make this occur routinely. Finally, the benefits of reduced inventories applies only to the future, so if the inventory is already plentiful for a particular item, reducing cycle time will affect responsiveness but not inventory.

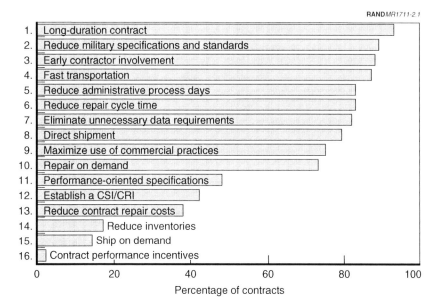

RAND*MR1711-2.1*

1. Long-duration contract
2. Reduce military specifications and standards
3. Early contractor involvement
4. Fast transportation
5. Reduce administrative process days
6. Reduce repair cycle time
7. Eliminate unnecessary data requirements
8. Direct shipment
9. Maximize use of commercial practices
10. Repair on demand
11. Performance-oriented specifications
12. Establish a CSI/CRI
13. Reduce contract repair costs
14. Reduce inventories
15. Ship on demand
16. Contract performance incentives

0   20   40   60   80   100
Percentage of contracts

NOTES: 26 percent of the contracts are from the U–2 Product Directorate. n = 101

Figure 2.1—Over 50 Percent of the Contracts in Our Sample Incorporated
10 of the 16 Innovations

CREP Tenet Groups: The Dependent Variables

As described in the last section, we grouped the CREP tenets into four policy-related groups and a fifth group that included all 16 CREP tenets. The four policy-related groups were: *simple modifications, key acquisition reform concepts, complete acquisition reform concepts,* and *agile logistics.* The fifth group—all 16 CREP tenets— was added for completeness to show whether tenets for both acquisition reform and agile logistics policies were being implemented. Each of the 101 sample contracts was evaluated according to these groups. The value of the dependent variable was the total number of tenets for a CREP innovation group that were incorporated in a contract.

We describe the four primary policy-relevant tenet groups below and provide the complete set of tenets.

- **Simple modifications:** Tenets that can be added to active contracts, usually related to speeding up transportation.

- **Key acquisition reform concepts:** The set of acquisition reform-related tenets that are clearly exhibited at the front of the contract (e.g., price and cycle time) and are relatively easy to measure.

- **Complete acquisition reform concepts:** All acquisition reform tenets included in the key acquisition reform group, plus those reform tenets not as easy to measure or identify consistently (e.g., maximize commercial practices).

- **Agile logistics:** All agile logistics or lean logistics tenets designed to reduce logistics pipelines by speeding up the repair and transportation segments of the pipeline as well as improving other logistics efficiencies (e.g., establish a CSI/CRI).

- **All CREP tenets:** These 16 tenets can also be found in the combined set of complete acquisition reform concepts and agile logistics.

Table 2.1 provides the particular tenets included in the first four groups of innovation policy objectives that we analyzed as dependent variables. The fifth group included all tenets. Figure 2.2 shows histograms of the variability in innovation across the five innovation groups or dependent variables.[11] Each histogram shows the percentage of contracts in our sample that included at least one tenet defined by our innovation group shown in Table 2.1.

One can observe in the first histogram in Figure 2.2 that most of the contracts in the sample (n = 101) included at least two *simple modifications* (that is, transportation-related) tenets.[12] The second

---

[11] The five most common tenets used were early contractor involvement, long-term contracts, reduction or elimination of military specifications, fast transportation, and the elimination of unnecessary data requirements.

[12] These tenets are included also in the simple modifications and agile logistics models.

Table 2.1

CREP Tenets Formed Four Primary Types of Innovation Groups

Tenets	Type of Innovation Groups			
	Simple Modification	Key AR Concepts	Complete AR	Agile Logistics
Reduce contract repair price		■	■	
Reduce repair cycle time		■		■
Reduce administrative process days			■	
Repair on demand				■
Establish a CSI/CRI				■
Direct shipment	■			■
Max use of commercial practices			■	
Performance-oriented specs		■	■	
Reduce inventories				■
Fast transportation	■			■
Ship on demand	■			■
Early contractor involvement		■	■	
Long-duration contract		■	■	
Reduce mil specs and stds			■	
Eliminate unnecessary data requirements			■	
Contract perform incentives		■	■	

histogram shows that the sample of contracts defined in the *key acquisition reform concepts* tenet group primarily incorporated between two and four acquisition reform tenets that were more objective to measure. The histogram labeled as *complete acquisition reform* shows that our sample of contracts typically incorporated seven or eight of the tenets involving acquisition reform. Most of the 101 contracts in our sample incorporated between three and five agile logistics tenets, shown by the histogram labeled *agile logistics*. Finally, our sample of contracts incorporated between 9 and 12 CREP tenets, shown in the last histogram labeled *all CREP tenets.*

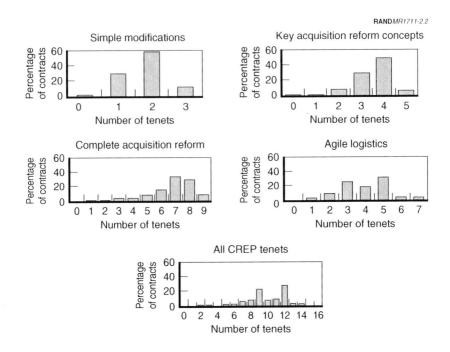

Figure 2.2—Number of Tenets Incorporated into CREP Contracts
by Tenet Group

Several tenets appear in more than one dependent variable; for example, the reduction in repair cycle time is an objective shared by both acquisition reform and agile logistics and appears in both dependent variables. Groups of tenets allowed us to ask whether organizational levers could help explain the types of broad policy objectives Warner Robins ALC set for CREP contracts, namely, *simple modifications, acquisition reform, agile logistics*, or *all of the above*.

REGRESSION ANALYSES

Each of the four tenet groups, plus the fifth, complete set of tenets, became a separate regression model. We analyzed the same set of 101 CREP contracts to determine the relationship organizational levers had with the incorporation of particular tenets in each of our defined tenet groups. According to information learned in interviews, CRTs were instructed by AFMC to apply as many of the CREP tenets as were appropriate in each contract.

In five separate multiple regression analyses, we regressed the groups of innovative contract types onto the nine organizational levers (see pages 17 to 25) and a U-2 Product Directorate dummy variable (see page 25). The dummy variable allowed us to account for any systematic differences between the U-2 contracts and the other 75 percent of the contracts in our sample.[13] Thus, we used regression analysis to explain how organizational levers were related to reported CREP innovation. A detailed description of the regression analyses and their results can be found in Appendix E. We discuss the results of our regression analyses in the next chapter.

SUMMARY OF METHODOLOGICAL APPROACH

As this chapter highlights, our study began with a literature review on organizational levers and innovation in the private sector. We used this information to structure interviews with personnel considered to have excelled at incorporating CREP tenets in the first CREP contracts. The literature review and interviews formed the basis for the survey of key personnel participating on contract repair teams, i.e., program managers, procurement contracting officers, production management specialists, and item management specialists. Using PCA, we identified and measured organizational levers from survey questions. Using AFMC data, we classified the total number of reported CREP tenets into five tenet groups: *simple modifications, key acquisition reform concepts, complete acquisition reform concepts, agile logistics,* and *all CREP tenets.* We then measured the use of these tenets in each of the 101 contracts in our sample. Finally, we regressed these CREP tenet groups on the organizational levers to determine the individual relationship each organizational lever had

---

[13]We refer the reader to Appendix E for regression analyses for CREP contracts minus the U-2 contracts (n = 75 contracts). The resulting set of models had less explanatory power for acquisition reform policy alternatives. Excluding U-2 contracts reduces the ratio between independent or predictor variables and sample size, which can cause variables to drop in significance. We caution the reader from drawing conclusions from this smaller sample. We include these analyses because the results isolate the effects of organizational variables on CRTs writing component repair contracts.

with the number of CREP tenets incorporated in the contract, hold-ing all other levers constant. The results of the regression analyses are discussed in the next chapter.

Chapter Three

MAIN FINDINGS AND IMPLICATIONS

This chapter presents the results of our regression analyses and discusses their primary implications for Air Force policy. The analyses were designed to measure the statistical relationship between the different organizational levers and operating-level personnel behavior. For a complete statistical account of the regression results, we refer the reader to Appendix E, which describes two sets of regression analyses of the innovation groups, one containing our complete sample of 101 Warner Robins ALC contracts and another sample set of only 75 Warner ALC contracts. The difference between the two groups is that the former includes U-2 Product Directorate sustainment contracts, which have repair components, whereas the latter contains only repair contracts. Of the two, the set of 101 contracts has greater statistical power because of its larger sample size. Thus, the discussion below considers regression analyses results only from the larger sample.

ORGANIZATIONAL LEVERS AND THEIR RELATIONSHIP WITH INNOVATION

Several patterns emerged from our regression analyses. First, the analyses provide empirical evidence that organizational levers show significant statistical relationships with reported contract innovation. People's behavior in incorporating tenets in contracts is associated with levers such as attitude toward acquisition reform, effective teaming, performance evaluation, and so on. This finding shows that policies and practices related to personnel behavior were a factor in the extent to which CRTs incorporated tenets in repair contracts.

Second, organizational levers appeared most statistically related to the implementation of agile logistics tenets, followed by simple modifications. Conversely, they were less associated with acquisition reform goals.

Training in acquisition reform consistently was related to reported tenet use. Training in acquisition reform had a statistically significant positive relationship with four contract innovation groups and the group of all CREP tenets. CRTs who reported more training in acquisition reform also incorporated more tenets. At the highest level of significance ($p < 0.01$), the analyses showed that as CRTs reported receiving more training in acquisition reform, they incorporated more tenets in the innovation groups of simple modifications, agile logistics, and all CREP tenets. At a slightly lower level of significance ($p < 0.05$), CRTs who reported more training in acquisition reform incorporated more tenets in the complete acquisition reform innovation group. Finally, at a still lower level of significance ($p < 0.10$), CRTs who reported more training in acquisition reform incorporated more tenets in key acquisition reform concepts. Personnel on CRTs who received more training used more tenets in their contracts, compared to personnel on CRTs with less training. Because of the constraints of the survey, we could not collect information on the quality of the training; however, given the consistent relationship between training and innovation and Air Force interest in further exploring quality in training and innovation, these results suggest that additional study is warranted.

Effective teaming had the second most consistent statistical relationship with contract innovation in all tenet groups, except simple modifications. However, the relationship between effective teaming and the extent of innovation for these groups was negative. In fact, effective teaming and the key acquisition reform concepts innovation group was the most statistically significant relationship ($p < 0.01$), followed by agile logistics and all CREP tenets ($p < 0.05$), and then by complete acquisition reform innovation ($p < 0.10$). We expected teams that considered themselves effective would write more innovative contracts. Surprisingly, the opposite relationship was found. The analyses indicate that as CRTs reported more problems with teaming, they implemented more tenets in their contracts compared with teams that reported higher team effectiveness scores.

Although not a statistically significant factor in terms of adopting a simple modifications model, the negative relationship is consistent.

While this negative relationship seems counterintuitive, we hypothesize that when contracting members worked as a team under CREP reform, rather than as individuals under the old process, members had to make consensus-like decisions in a new way that required more give and take. Perhaps teams that pushed reform further pressured its members to learn new practices, take more risks, work longer hours, and spend more time trying to bring around the skeptics among its members. Perhaps innovation is occurring by fiat over the objections of other team members, leading to a sense that the team is not unified in purpose or direction. On the other hand, teams that reported an easier teaming experience may have settled for less aggressive goals. In retrospect, it is not surprising that the teaming variable was not related to the simple modification goals, because these innovations, which are simpler to incorporate and change little of the basic contractor-Air Force relationship, do not involve as much creative problem solving among team members as other goals.

A study conducted by Gerald Miller (1993) may further explain these counterintuitive findings. In a study of the relationship between team stability and learning among work teams, Miller found that unstable teams—teams whose members changed frequently—experienced higher learning rates when confronted with new problems. Work team instability encouraged members to expand alternatives and solutions. He also found that unstable teams required more complex management arrangements to keep team members on track.

The negative relationship may also be a result of the question wording in the survey. The survey asked about end-state conditions of teaming effectiveness, such as the effectiveness of the CRT to overcome barriers to cooperation or the extent to which team members worked toward a common goal. Constraints on our survey did not allow us to pursue the exact nature of CRT teamwork processes or attitude measures, such as group dynamics. Future research might clarify this.

Ultimately, the negative effective teaming result was perhaps our most surprising and potentially troublesome finding. If these negative experiences continue—and we do not know if they have because this study ended not long after the end of the CREP initiative—teams may opt for less innovation if smoother team dynamics are preferred. This result strongly suggests that AFMC and the ALCs will want to investigate teaming more thoroughly.

Attitude toward acquisition reform had the third most consistent statistical relationship with contract innovation. It had a statistically significant positive relationship in each innovation group except for key acquisition reform concepts. The regression analyses showed, with a high level of significance ($p < 0.05$), a positive relationship between attitude toward acquisition reform and simple modifications and all CREP tenets innovation groups. A positive relationship between team member attitude toward acquisition reform and the incorporation of tenets in the complete acquisition reform and agile logistics innovation groups had a slightly lower level of significance ($p < 0.10$). These results suggest that those CRTs that view reform more positively are associated with greater implementation of reform tenets in their contracts. One can also think about attitude as an approximate measure of operating-level "buy-in." Those teams that agree with the goals of the initiative are associated with more innovative contracts.

Contractor partnering showed a positive relationship with tenets implemented for simple modifications and agile logistics goals. This result indicates that those CRTs that included more reform tenets in contracts also perceived contractors to be better partners. The significance level for the positive relationship between contractor partnering and the incorporation of tenets in an innovation group was highest with simple modifications ($p < 0.01$) and slightly less with agile logistics ($p < 0.05$). This result is encouraging, but the relationship is not statistically significant for either of the two acquisition reform models or for the model including all CREP tenets.

Leadership consistency was statistically significant only in the agile logistics ($p < 0.01$) and key acquisition reform ($p < 0.05$) innovation models. Leadership consistency had a positive, significant relationship with CRT incorporation of agile logistics and key acquisition reform tenets. CRTs that perceived consistent messages throughout management and that believed reform would be around for some time were associated with the incorporation of these types of tenets in their contracts. According to Larkin and Larkin (1994), rank-and-file employees listen to their first-level supervisors and not just senior leadership. These employees need to hear about change repeatedly from their supervisors before they believe the change effort will have staying power. If supervisors are not committed to change, Larkin and Larkin found it is very difficult for them to win over rank-and-file employees. The survey in our study did not ask questions about middle management as an organizational lever, but the results suggest it warrants further consideration.

Performance evaluation had a negative statistical relationship with agile logistics tenets ($p < 0.05$). One would typically expect this organizational lever to have a positive relationship with innovation, so we found these results surprising and deserving of attention. The analysis indicates that those CRTs that said they were more likely to be graded on improving the timeliness of the contracts they processed, working effectively with other team members, improving contract performance, and improving partnering with contractors were less likely to incorporate agile logistics reform tenets. In addition, our results indicate no relationship between performance evaluation and the other tenet models. To explain these results, we hypothesize that those CRT members who are more likely to succeed in writing innovative contracts feel they will not be rewarded sufficiently for their effort.[1] If correct, it suggests that the ALCs will need to align performance evaluation criteria more closely to desired new behavior, to apply perhaps to all team members.

Job experience showed a negative statistical significance for the simple modifications and complete acquisition reform innovation groups ($p < 0.10$). It had no relationship with the other two innovation groups or the complete set of tenets. The negative relationship indicates that CRTs included slightly more transportation-related (simple modifications) tenets to contracts as the level of personnel experience decreased. However, the magnitude of its relationship

---

[1] Our results suggest that the ALCs might want to align performance incentives with other contracting-related initiatives, if they have not done so already, and include criteria explicitly designed to reinforce CRT contract innovation.

with the incorporation of reform tenets is so slight as to have little practical consequence.

Two variables—**performance incentives** and **Air Force partnering**— had no explanatory power in any of the models we tested. Senior leadership indicated Warner Robins ALC has systematically and intensively tried to provide nonmonetary rewards for writing particularly innovative contracts. Perhaps the types of incentives specified in our survey were not sufficiently representative of rewards offered or perhaps personnel do not perceive these rewards as effective. We were somewhat surprised by the lack of explanatory power for Air Force partnering. It suggests that there is no consistent relationship between the role of the Air Force as customer and the number of innovative tenets included in repair contracts. This study could not delve into the complex issues involved in how the Air Force works with its suppliers. More attention needs to be given to this important issue. Many ongoing transformation initiatives, such as purchasing and supply chain management (PSCM), corporate contracting, and strategic sourcing, depend on effective contractor and Air Force partnering.

Finally, the **U-2 Product Directorate** dummy variable showed statistical significance with every innovation group except simple modifications. We included this variable to account for the important differences between sustainment and component repair contracts and their respective contracting processes and environment. The dummy variable accounts generally for binary differences within a sample set, in this case, sustainment versus repair contracts. Holding all other organizational levers constant, the dummy variable showed that the U-2 directorate incorporated more tenets in the complete acquisition reform, agile logistics, and all CREP tenet groups ($p < 0.01$). The U-2 directorate also incorporated more key acquisition reform tenets with a slightly lower significance level ($p < 0.05$). At the time of this study, the U-2 Product Directorate reported a high rate of tenet use, which has been substantiated in follow-up discussions at Warner Robins ALC.

LESSONS FOR THE AIR FORCE

In general, the results suggest that the Air Force should continue to make effective use of those organizational levers associated with positive results, especially training in and fostering positive attitudes toward acquisition reform. In turn, it should revisit the levers associated with null or negative relationships, especially performance evaluation and teaming. Specifically, the Air Force could do more to

- Inform personnel that senior leadership wants to see progress in achieving well-specified contracting goals.

- Learn how to create effective teams through training in group problem-solving and working with others from different functional backgrounds, in addition to educating teams on legal and policy changes.

- Align personal evaluation criteria and incentives to reform goals.

EXTENDING THESE RESULTS TO OTHER AIR FORCE INITIATIVES

To the degree that the CREP initiative is representative of contract reform efforts in general, the Air Force can reinforce the organizational levers related to innovation and look closely at those that seem unrelated or are negatively related.

Are the lessons from this study applicable to other ALCs? The answer depends on how similar the CREP initiative at Warner Robins ALC is, in terms of the organizational context and policy goals, to other initiatives and at other locations. We hypothesize that it is reasonable to think the relationship between organizational levers and contract innovation at Warner Robins ALC is similar to the relationship of these variables at both Oklahoma City and Ogden ALCs. However, it is also possible, because this study analyzed contracts at a center viewed by HQ AFMC as innovative, that these results would not apply to the other two centers. Also, senior leadership at the other ALCs may have had a different impact on personnel behavior at their centers. One would have to conduct a similar analysis at these centers to know conclusively whether organizational levers could help explain innovation at those sites.[2]

---

[2]The inclusion of those two centers probably would have increased the sample size enough to allow for dummy variables to represent the respective centers. We tried at one point to expand this study to include contracts written at other Air Logistics

Could the same relationship between levers and innovation that we find under the CREP initiative occur with other contract initiatives? After all, the Air Force has taken on other contracting-related initiatives since CREP, many of which attempt more significant change in behaviors and even organizational structure, such as the PSCM initiative.[3] If senior leadership does not address the levers identified as having no relationship or having a negative relationship with innovation implementation, then leadership may have to work as diligently—or more diligently, depending on the initiative—to implement new innovative practices, much as it did for CREP.

This study should help leadership consider the behavioral implications of contracting initiatives such as CREP and decide what to do if it wants personnel to implement contract innovation. This study also provides an analytical approach to measuring the relationship between organizational levers and forms of contract innovation other than CREP. Since this study began, the Air Force has added initiatives that are more complicated than CREP in their approach and expected outcomes, such as PSCM, corporate contracting, and performance-based contracting. The need to encourage new approaches and reinforce desired behavior at the ALCs is important to the success of the Air Force's ongoing transformation efforts—a process in which support at the operating level is essential. As such, the Air Force may want to apply this methodology to other initiatives where behavioral changes are needed to fulfill larger transformational goals.

Centers to capture potential item and cultural differences at Oklahoma City and Ogden ALCs, but repair workload backlogs in 1998 and 1999 prevented the other ALCs from participating.

[3]The PSCM initiative, demonstrated on the F100 engine at Oklahoma City ALC in FY2002, has as its objective a strategic means of selecting and managing suppliers to provide more effective and efficient support to the warfighter. While consistent with CREP outcome goals, it would work with purchasing and supply chain activities from an enterprise-level to an operating-level perspective. Behavioral implications for PSCM are more significant than for CREP.

REPAIR PRICE AND NEGOTIATED FLOW DAY DIFFERENCES IN WARNER ROBINS ALC CREP AND NON-CREP CONTRACTS

In a separate analysis that complements this study, we examined whether CREP made a difference in contract performance outcomes, specifically, in repair prices and negotiated flow days (the repair cycle time required by a contract).[1] The question of whether the initiative leads to a measurable improvement in outcomes was of interest to the Air Force. The results described in this Appendix suggest that CREP repair contracts written by Warner Robins ALC during the initial phase of CREP reduced repair cycle time without increasing unit repair prices.

The analysis described here collected data on CREP and non-CREP contracts, i.e., contracts written during the same period as CREP but that did not use the CREP process. We also collected data on contracts directly preceding CREP to compare item prices and negotiated flow days on CREP-period contracts with prices and flow days for the same items on the just-expired, old contracts. This method allowed us to control for technical differences across items while comparing changes in price and flow days.

In sum, we found that CREP contracts reduced flow days without increases to unit repair price in comparison with non-CREP contracts written in the same period. Non-CREP contracts also had reduced

---

[1] Negotiated flow days or repair cycle time is the time from an item's induction into repair to its completed repair.

flow days compared with previous contracts, but unit repair prices increased. The statistical analyses that follow help to explain these findings.

Data from the Contract Depot Maintenance Production and Cost System (G072D) identified the old contract number for items on CREP and non-CREP contracts through the National Item Identification Number (NIIN). The CREP metrics worksheet Warner Robins ALC supplied to HQ AFMC provided CREP contract numbers. Non-CREP contracts were those repair contracts written during the CREP initiative that Warner Robins ALC did not classify as CREP. Only those NIINs on the CREP and non-CREP contracts that replaced a recently expired, old contract became part of the analysis. Changes in prices and flow days for CREP and non-CREP items were compared between the old and new contracts. Some NIINs had more than one just-expired contract written within the same year. A NIIN could have several CREP contracts if the first contract was written or modified early in the initiative.

Warner Robins ALC provided copies of contracts for the CREP and non-CREP contract pairs identified from G072D.[2] The analysis considered only items that had nonzero entries for items repaired, scheduled inputs, and repair price. All price-related data were converted into constant dollars (base year 2000) using Secretary of the Air Force Financial Management price deflators.

In all, G072D provided data on 375 unique NIINs from 182 contracts that had repairs on CREP and non-CREP contracts written during the CREP initiative and their respective older contracts. Some NIINs appeared on several CREP contracts, but all pairs of contract/NIIN data were unique. These unique pairs of contract comparisons produced 319 observations for CREP NIINs and 135 observations for non-CREP NIINs. This sample consisted of 48 CREP contracts paired with 60 older contracts and 30 non-CREP contracts paired with 44 older contracts. The data set included 48 of the 74 CREP contracts

---

[2]The contract office, headed by Jim Grant, provided this study significant assistance by copying 297 repair contracts. We extracted data from those contracts and continually referred to them to clear up questions raised by data ambiguities in other information systems.

reported to HQ AFMC or 65 percent of those awarded and reported to G072D as of September 1998.[3]

PRICE AND NEGOTIATED FLOW DAY DIFFERENCES FOR CREP AND NON-CREP ITEMS

The results of these comparisons of price and schedule are shown in Figures A.1 to A.4. Figure A.1 compares prices for NIINs (n = 319) from 48 CREP contracts with their just-expired, old contracts. About 66 percent of the CREP sample of NIINs shows a reduction in repair prices.[4] On average, prices decreased by three percent. Half of the sample had repair price improvements of less than or equal to 18 percent. Over 8 percent of the sample showed price increases over 100 percent. Changes in contract design may account for most of the large increases in this comparison. Some contracts went from firm-fixed price to cost-plus-fixed-fee. Others had CREP contracts with a few NIINs, but the older contract had many NIINs.

The non-CREP sample of 135 NIINs came from 30 contracts. Figure A.2 shows that 62 percent of the non-CREP NIINs had repair price improvements, but the scale of those improvements differed greatly from CREP NIINs. On average, repair prices for the non-CREP sample of NIINs increased by 12 percent compared with their old contracts. Half of the NIINs in our sample showed repair price reductions of four percent or more, with very few NIINs exhibiting reductions greater than 20 percent. Over 30 percent of the non-CREP NIINs had virtually no change in unit repair prices.

---

[3]In September 1998, Warner Robins ALC reported that 101 contracts had incorporated one or more CREP tenets during the CREP initiative. Of those 101 contracts, 27 were written by the U-2 Product Directorate and primarily classified. We included U-2 contracts in the behavioral model, because the CREP tenets incorporated in those contracts were available and we were able to survey the appropriate personnel. The data set for the comparison of prices and schedule for items before and after the CREP initiative was restricted to the set of 74 unclassified contracts written by "non-U-2"product directorates for obvious reasons having to do with data availability and reporting requirements. Unclassified repair contracts paid for by the revolving fund get reported to G072D.

[4]Repair prices excluded government-furnished materiel (GFM) costs.

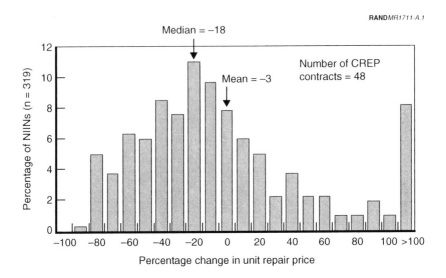

Figure A.1—Sixty-Six Percent of CREP Sample NIINs Showed Reduced Unit Repair Prices

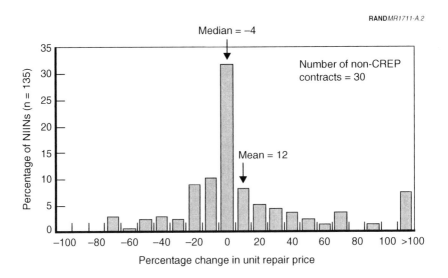

Figure A.2—Sixty-Two Percent of Non-CREP NIINs Showed Improved Unit Repair Prices, But On Average Prices Increased

The next two figures compare flow days. Figure A.3 shows the negotiated flow days for the same sample of CREP NIINs (n = 319). This sample revealed impressive improvement—58 percent of the sample exhibited improvements in negotiated flow days. On average, CREP NIIN negotiated flow days decreased by 14 percent or more. Half of the CREP sample showed flow day reductions of 23 percent or more.

Figure A.4 indicates that 60 percent of the non-CREP NIINs in our sample had reduced negotiated flow days. In fact, on average, negotiated flow days decreased by 24 percent for our non-CREP sample of NIINs. Half of the sample showed flow day reductions of 20 percent or more.

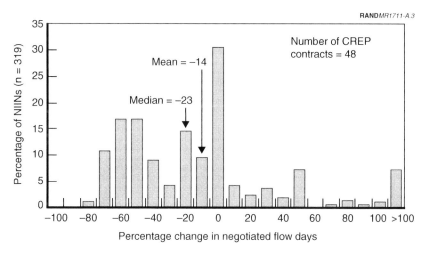

Figure A.3—Fifty-Eight Percent of CREP Sample NIINs Also Showed
Reduced Negotiated Flow Days

STATISTICAL ANALYSES OF PRICE AND NEGOTIATED FLOW DAY DIFFERENCES

Are these results statistically meaningful? To examine this question, we tested whether the percentage changes for CREP and non-CREP were different from one another. We also tested whether CREP and

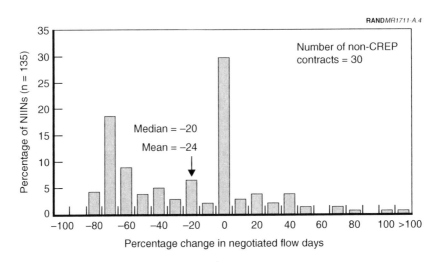

Figure A.4—Sixty Percent of Non-CREP Sample NIINs Showed Improved Negotiated Flow Days

non-CREP price and flow days were different from previous contract values, i.e., were the percentage changes different from zero? We used two-tailed t-tests to evaluate differences. Table A.1 shows the CREP and non-CREP repair price and flow day values used in our analyses.

Table A.1

Repair Price and Negotiated Flow Day Statistics for CREP and Non-CREP Items

	CREP items (N = 319)	Non-CREP items (N = 135)	CREP vs. Non-CREP Tests
Repair price (% change)			
Average	–3.20	11.81*	*
Standard deviation	(69.78)	(62.35)	
Negotiated flow days (% change)			
Average	–13.74***	–23.85***	*
Standard deviation	(54.94)	45.21	

NOTE: Asterisks indicate significant differences from previous contracts: * denotes $p < 0.05$; ** denotes $p < 0.01$; *** denotes $p < 0.001$.

Prices

A t-test evaluating differences between CREP and non-CREP percentage change in price was significant (t = 2.26, p < 0.02). The means indicate that CREP price changes (average percentage change = –3.20) were smaller than non-CREP price changes (average percentage change = 11.81). However, CREP repair prices were not significantly different from older contracts, i.e., they were essentially unchanged (t = 0.82, p > 0.05). On the other hand, non-CREP prices were significantly different from older contracts (t = 2.23, p < 0.05). These results indicate that mean CREP repair prices were not significantly different from mean prices for the same items on previous, older contracts. Non-CREP repair prices were significantly different, with higher mean prices for items on non-CREP contracts compared with the same items on older contracts. Thus, while repair prices were statistically unchanged for CREP, they were higher with non-CREP contract items.

Next, we discuss differences in schedule or negotiated flow days for these contracts, comparing old and new contracts for the same items.

Negotiated Flow Days

A t-test evaluating the difference between CREP and non-CREP percentage change in flow days was significant (t = 2.01, p < 0.05). The means indicate that the percentage decreases in non-CREP flow days (average = –23.85) were greater than percentage decreases in CREP flow days (average = –13.74). Both CREP and non-CREP items had significant decreases in flow days from previous contracts (CREP: t = 4.46, p < 0.001; non-CREP: t = 6.13, p < 0.001). These results indicate that both CREP and non-CREP contracts showed improvements in schedules compared with their previous contracts.

In sum, the data indicate that the CREP initiative was successful at holding prices constant over time while reducing flow days. Reduction of flow days across both CREP and non-CREP contracts was strong, but price increased with improved schedule, except where CREP was implemented. We hypothesize that the primary effect of

CREP was to minimize price increases while reducing negotiated flow days, an explicit goal of agile logistics and the primary thrust of the CREP initiative at Warner Robins ALC.

INTERVIEW QUESTIONS FOR CONTRACT REPAIR TEAMS

The study team interviewed individuals who had participated in Contract Repair Teams (CRTs) or Integrated Product Teams (IPTs) for CREP contracts. Those people interviewed were identified by Warner Robins-ALC/PK and Warner Robins-ALC/RE as innovative in incorporating CREP tenets in repair contracts. Individuals, who were interviewed in groups, were sent questions before the meetings. The questions were structured but somewhat open-ended. They were meant to guide discussions, although participants were encouraged to volunteer issues the researchers had not anticipated. The interviews influenced the kinds of questions our survey included and their wording.

The interview questions for the April 1998 and June 1998 interviews are as follows. The CRT participants were asked to answer the questions in light of a specific contract the ALC considered most innovative or successful in incorporating CREP tenets.

- Contract background

- Contract number

- Contractor name

- Number of contract line items (CLINs)

- Contract duration (base year plus number of options)

- Dollar amount (estimated)

- Contract type

- Repair material used (government-furnished material [GFM] or contractor-furnished material [CFM]).

Initial process steps

- Requirements determination/identification

  - What role does the Program Manager play in this process?

  - Was the list of National Stock Numbers (NSNs) in the CREP contract similar to the previous contract(s)?

  - How did acquisition reform/lean logistics or other CREP tenets affect this part of the process?

  - Was a Statement of Objective used or a Statement of Work?

  - Was there early contractor involvement?

- Purchase Request (PR) package

  - Primary milestones (date started and completed)

- Funding

  - What funding issues were involved with the CRT's ability to achieve the contract design goal (the lay-in of long-lead-time parts/rotable pool, etc.)?

CRT/IPT

- Who initiated the CRT or IPT and why?

- Who were the core members?

- How often did the team meet?

- Was there an advantage to using a CRT? Disadvantages?

- Were the Defense Contract Audit Agency (DCAA) and the Defense Contract Management Agency (DCMC) directly involved?

- How did the contractor participate?

- Did all members of the CRT work toward a common goal? Were there conflicts between CRT and functional goals? If so, how were they resolved?

Contract design

- In what major ways is this contract different from its predecessor?

- What innovations were incorporated in the contract? Improvements?

- What other innovations were contemplated but not incorporated?

- How was the acquisition strategy determined? Based on what goals?

- What were the primary challenges in contract design? How were they overcome?

- Was a cost benefit analysis conducted? If so, what were the results and how did they influence contract design?

- Was market research conducted? If so, what sources were consulted and who performed the analyses?

- What major "firsts" were accomplished in this contract or during the process?

Lessons learned

- What did the CRT learn from this contract experience?

- Did the CRT consult with other sources to learn from others before writing this contract? If so, what sources were consulted?

- Have the lessons learned from this contract influenced the way other contracts were written? If so, which ones and how?

CREP SURVEY CONDUCTED AT WARNER ROBINS ALC

The CREP survey conducted at Warner Robins ALC in 1998 and 1999 appears in the next six pages. Key participants in the contract repair teams (program managers, procurement contracting officers, production management specialists, and item management specialists) or those individuals who had most influence on the requirements and contract design steps of the CREP process filled out the survey online and submitted it to RAND electronically. The survey was conducted in 1998 and again in 1999 with CRT individuals who had not completed the survey the first time. Questions 24 to 44 were based on issues arising from acquisition reform and agile logistics that concerned individual behavior and factors that affected behavior.[1] Thus, they applied generally to all of the CREP contracts in which the individual had participated. The survey questions that follow provided the data for the organizational levers or independent variables. The survey is shown as it appeared to Warner Robins ALC survey participants.

---

[1]Questions 1 to 23 (not shown) pertained to individual contracts and the contracting process. These responses were too incomplete to use in the study and were dropped from further consideration.

**Implementing Acquisition Reform in Depot Maintenance Contracts:
Survey of Warner Robins ALC**

Your Name: [   ]

A. Attitude toward Acquisition Reform

24. How well do you understand the goals of acquisition reform?

Very well	Well	Somewhat well	Not well	Not at all well
O	O	O	O	O

25. How supportive are you of the goals of acquisition reform?

Very supportive	Supportive	Somewhat supportive	Not supportive	Not at all supportive
O	O	O	O	O

26. How likely is acquisition reform to contribute to the following outcomes (*check all that apply*)?

Outcome	Very likely	Likely	Somewhat likely	Not likely	Not at all likely
Improve mission capability rates for end user	O	O	O	O	O
Reduce the cost of my contracts	O	O	O	O	O
Increase contractor responsiveness/flexibility	O	O	O	O	O
Increase my workload	O	O	O	O	O
Increase my job satisfaction	O	O	O	O	O
Make my job more secure	O	O	O	O	O

B. Leadership

27. How supportive of acquisition reform are the following individuals or groups?

Individual/Group	Very supportive	Supportive	Somewhat supportive	Not supportive	Not at all Supportive
Headquarters AFMC	O	O	O	O	O
Your ALC leadership	O	O	O	O	O
Your product directorate leadership	O	O	O	O	O
Your immediate supervisor	O	O	O	O	O

28. How true are the following statements about acquisition reform?

Statement	Very true	True	Somewhat true	Not true	Not at all true
Air Force leadership has made a strong case for why we need acquisition reform.	O	O	O	O	O
Different parts of the chain of command send different messages about acquisition reform	O	O	O	O	O
Management attitudes suggest that acquisition reform is the latest "program of the month."	O	O	O	O	O
I would be punished for a failed attempt to do something innovative with a contract.	O	O	O	O	O
I would be rewarded for a successful attempt to do something innovative with a contract.	O	O	O	O	O
Hard work integrating acquisition reform into a contract goes unnoticed by management.	O	O	O	O	O

C. Performance Evaluation and Rewards

29. How important are the following factors in your yearly performance evaluation?

Factor	Very important	Important	Somewhat Important	Not Important	Not at all important
Increasing the number of all types of contracts processed	O	O	O	O	O
Increasing the number of commercial contracts processed	O	O	O	O	O
Improving the timeliness of contracts process (reduced administrative lead time)	O	O	O	O	O
Working effectively with the members of my CRT	O	O	O	O	O
Improving contract performance (cost, reliability, cycle times)	O	O	O	O	O
Improving my educational qualifications	O	O	O	O	O
Improving partnering with contractors	O	O	O	O	O

30. How likely is the effective use of acquisition reform to lead to the following rewards?

Reward	Very likely	Likely	Somewhat likely	Not likely	Not at all likely
Higher merit increases	O	O	O	O	O
Improved opportunities for promotion	O	O	O	O	O
Non-monetary rewards (e.g., time off, trips)	O	O	O	O	O
Recognition from ALC/product directorate/division for a job well done	O	O	O	O	O
Official acknowledgment of customer satisfaction	O	O	O	O	O

D. Teaming and Partnering

31. How many CRTs (or contract IPTs) have you participated in this fiscal year? [   ]

32. How true are the following statements about the CRTs (or IPTs) you have worked on?

Statement	Very true	True	Somewhat true	Not true	Not at all true
The CRT was effective in overcoming functional or disciplinary barriers to cooperation.	O	O	O	O	O
Some team members had a poor understanding of acquisition reform.	O	O	O	O	O
Team members worked toward a common performance goal.	O	O	O	O	O
Non-core CRT members (FM, BC, CR, EN, QA) were well integrated into the process	O	O	O	O	O

33. How effective and responsive were the following individuals or groups in completing their tasks for the CRTs (or IPTs) you have worked on?

Individual/Group	Very effective	Effective	Somewhat effectiv	Not effective	Not at all effective
Program Manager/Logistics Officer	O	O	O	O	O
Item Manager	O	O	O	O	O
Production Management Specialist	O	O	O	O	O
Procurement Contracting Officer	O	O	O	O	O
Equipment Specialist	O	O	O	O	O
Engineering	O	O	O	O	O
Quality Assurance	O	O	O	O	O
Financial Management	O	O	O	O	O
Contract DMAG	O	O	O	O	O
Competition Advocate	O	O	O	O	O
Small Business	O	O	O	O	O
Acquisition Support Team (AST), formerly known as the RFP Support Office (RFPSO)	O	O	O	O	O

34. **How true are the following statements about the relationship between the Air Force and contractors for the contracts you have worked on?**

Statement	Very true	True	Somewhat true	Not true	Not at all true
A positive working relationship exists with the contractors	O	O	O	O	O
The Air Force and contractors have worked together to improve processes and reduce cycle time.	O	O	O	O	O
Contractors alert the Air Force to anticipated problems that could affect the contractor's performance.	O	O	O	O	O
Contractors show a willingness to assume risks in order to do business with the Air Force.	O	O	O	O	O
The Air Force shows a willingness to pay for the risks it wants contractors to assume.	O	O	O	O	O
The Air Force shows a commitment to reward contractors who perform well.	O	O	O	O	O

E. Training and Career Development

35. - 38. **How many years of work experience do you have in**

	your present job?	[ ]
	the Air Force?	[ ]
other non Air Force government positions?		[ ]
	the private sector?	[ ]

39. - 40. What is your current GS grade and step?

GS grade: [   ]

GS step: [   ]

41. About how many days of formal training in acquisition reform have you received in the past two fiscal years?
O None
O 1 to 2 weeks
O 3 to 4 weeks
O More than one month

42. How often do you receive formal or informal training updates on acquisition reform as it affects your job?
O Weekly
O Monthly
O Quarterly
O Biannually
O Annually
O Less than once a year

43. In what areas is a lack of training for you or your colleagues slowing the implementation of acquisition reform (*check all that apply*)?

☐ Requirements determination
☐ Market research
☐ Seeking industry input into RFP development
☐ Determining price reasonableness
☐ Developing the PR package as well as contract terms and conditions
☐ Negotiation of contract terms and conditions
☐ None of the above

44. How important are the following sources of information for keeping current changes and "best practices" in contracting?

Factor	Very important	Important	Somewhat Important	Not Important	Not at all important
DoD Acquisition Reform Web site	O	O	O	O	O
My ALC Web site	O	O	O	O	O
Web sites at other ALCs or Headquarters AFMC	O	O	O	O	O
The "home office" for my function at the ALC	O	O	O	O	O
The Acquisition Support Team (aka RFPSO) at the ALC	O	O	O	O	O
Other personnel in my product directorate or at ALC	O	O	O	O	O
Contractors	O	O	O	O	O
Official memos, newsletters, and videos	O	O	O	O	O
Roadshows or Acquisition Reform Stand-down Week	O	O	O	O	O

Submit   If you have any questions or experience problems, please contact Mary Chenoweth by e-mail (mec@rand.org) or telephone (310-393-0411, x6248).

ORGANIZATIONAL LEVER VARIABLES FROM SURVEY DATA: PRINCIPAL COMPONENTS ANALYSES

The goal of the principal components analyses (PCAs) was to identify the key organizational lever factors that could be described by a linear combination of survey questions. PCAs allow one to examine relationships among responses to determine whether particular questions reflect the same underlying concept. These analyses permit data from numerous questions or items to be classified into a few factors that describe unique scales. PCAs, rather than factor analyses, are an appropriate technique to use when the analyses are exploratory in nature and one wants to account for total variance instead of shared variance. PCA is particularly appropriate here, because we had no prior experience with how people would respond to or interpret the survey questions. PCA is a technique commonly used in psychology in the development of scales of personality and intelligence (Tabachnick and Fidell, 1996).

Based on theoretical assumptions about what the survey was trying to measure, data were analyzed separately for questions addressing different organizational levers.[1] We conducted eight different PCAs to identify eight lever variables and then computed two others directly (i.e., not using PCA)—job experience and a product directorate dummy variable. PCA fundamentally assumes that all the responses

---

[1]PCAs conducted on all 29 question subparts created factors similar to those based on eight separate PCA analyses. These results indicate that the survey respondents perceived our theoretical concepts as separate or distinct factors.

are measured on a similar continuous scale (e.g., five-point scales). The PCA technique identified eight organizational lever factors:

- Attitude toward acquisition reform

- Leadership consistency

- Performance evaluations

- Performance incentives

- Effective teaming

- Contractor partnering

- Air Force partnering

- Training in acquisition reform.

This study used PCA with varimax rotation using Kaiser's eigenvalue rule (Nunnally, 1978), which states that only factors with eigenvalues greater than one are retained. This rule means that only factors that explain more variance than a single item are computed. Eigenvalues express how much variance is explained by each factor; principal components compute factors so that the first factor represents the largest amount of variance. The correlation between the factor and specific items is reported by the factor loading of each item. The amount by which each variable "loads" on a factor is measured by its correlation with the component. Using a cutoff value of 0.60, survey items with high factor loadings were retained for further analyses, except for the training in acquisition reform variable where the two items were not highly correlated (see Table D.1).[2] The regression analyses retained the training in acquisition reform variable even though it failed to meet the cutoff criteria because of its importance in implementing new business practices.

Varimax rotation maximizes the variance of the squared loadings and is the most common orthogonal rotation method (DeVellis, 1991).

---

[2]Items related to job experience and training did not load on the same factor. Because we were interested in the relationship of both job experience (i.e., number of years in present job) and the amount of training Air Force personnel had received with contract innovation, items from both training and job experience were retained as distinct organizational levers, and thus independent variables for the multiple regression analyses.

Rotated factor patterns and Cronbach's coefficient alphas (Cronbach, 1951) were computed for each factor. Cronbach's coefficient alpha is a widely used measure of reliability in which alpha signifies one minus the error variance. Thus, high reliability is denoted by alpha values close to one. Table D.1 shows the results of the PCAs in identifying survey questions by organizational lever.

Table D.1

Organization Levers Measured by Survey Questions

Organizational Lever	Factor Loading	Alpha
1. Attitude toward acquisition reform		0.887
How supportive are you of the goals of acquisition reform? (Q25)	0.694	
How likely is acquisition reform to contribute to the following outcomes? (Q26)		
• Improve mission capability rates for end user	0.833	
• Reduce the cost of my contracts	0.807	
• Increase contractor responsiveness/flexibility	0.872	
• Increase my job satisfaction	0.907	
• Make my job more secure	0.684	
2. Leadership consistency		0.625
How true are the following statements about acquisition reform? (Q28)		
• Different parts of the chain of command send different messages about acquisition reform	0.853	
• Management attitudes suggest that acquisition reform is the latest "program of the month"	0.853	
3. Performance evaluations		0.887
How important are the following factors in your yearly performance evaluation? (Q29)		
• Improving the timeliness of contracts processed (reduced administrative lead-time)	0.843	
• Working effectively with the members of my CRT	0.824	
• Improving contract performance (cost, reliability, cycle times)	0.913	
• Improving partnering with contractors	0.877	

Table D.1 (continued)

Organizational Lever	Factor Loading	Alpha
4. Performance incentives		0.901
How likely is the effective use of acquisition reform to lead to the following rewards? (Q30)		
• Higher merit increases	0.873	
• Improved opportunities for promotion	0.912	
• Non-monetary rewards (e.g., time off, trips)	0.863	
• Recognition from ALC/product directorate/division of a job well done	0.776	
• Official acknowledgment of customer satisfaction	0.811	
5. Effective teaming		0.678
How true are the following statements about the CRTs (or IPTs) you have worked on? (Q32)		
• The CRT was effective in overcoming functional or disciplinary barriers to cooperation.	0.846	
• Team members worked toward a common performance goal.	0.801	
• Non-core CRT members (FM, BC, CR, EN, QA) were well integrated into the process.	0.689	
6. Contractor partnering		0.873
How true are the following statements about the relationship between the Air Force and the contractor? (Q34)		
• A positive working relationship exists with the contractor.	0.875	
• The Air Force and contractor have worked together to improve processes and reduce cycle time.	0.859	
• The contractor alerts the Air Force to anticipated problems that could affect the contractor's performance.	0.864	
• The contractor shows a willingness to assume risks in order to do business with the Air Force.	0.805	
7. Air Force partnering		0.718
How true are the following statements about the relationship between the Air Force and the contractor? (Q34)		
• The Air Force shows a willingness to pay for the risks it wants the contractor to assume.	0.883	
• The Air Force shows a commitment to reward contractors who perform well.	0.883	

Table D.1 (continued)

Organizational Lever	Factor Loading	Alpha
8. Training in acquisition reform		0.392
How many days of formal training in acquisition reform have you received in the past two fiscal years? (Q41)	0.789	
How often do you receive formal and informal training updates on acquisition reform as it affects your job? (Q42)	0.789	
9. Job experience		n/a
How many years of work experience do you have in your current job? (Q35)		
10. U-2 Product Directorate		n/a

STATISTICAL RESULTS OF THE MULTIVARIATE ANALYSES

INTRODUCTION

This appendix gives the results of an ordinary least squares (OLS) regression with the four CREP innovation groups and the fifth group that includes all CREP tenets as the dependent measures. We show two sets of results for all analyses. The first half of Table E.1 gives the results of the five regression models using 101 observations, which include component repair and U-2 sustainment contracts. The second half of the table shows the results for the sample of just the component repair contracts (without U-2 sustainment contracts, n = 75). Our dependent measure is the number of innovation group tenets incorporated in the contract sample. The analyses regressed the dependent variable, i.e., the number of tenets, onto the organizational lever variables. Appendix C described how the survey questions were used to construct the organizational lever variables.

Because our dependent variables in each of the five groups were not continuous, but rather limited in range, probit analyses were also performed. The probit results were strikingly similar to the results of the OLS analyses and indicate that our conclusions are robust across both estimation methods. The OLS analyses offer results that are

Table E.1

Results from the OLS Regression Analyses: Standardized Coefficients (β) by Contract Innovation Group

Organizational Levers	Contract Innovation Groups (n = 101; component repair and sustainment contracts)					Contract Innovation Groups (n = 75; component repair contracts only)				
	Simple Mods	Key AR Concepts	Complete AR	Agile Logistics	All CREP Tenets	Simple Mods	Key AR Concepts	Complete AR	Agile Logistics	All CREP Tenets
Intercept	0.28	3.82	7.28	1.19	7.38	1.03	3.97	8.58	2.18	9.57
Attitude toward AR[a]	0.39	0.31	0.83	0.52	1.27	0.75	0.23	1.41	0.81	2.20
Leadership consistency[a]	0.20	0.32	0.32	0.44	0.64	-0.01	0.33	0.07	0.17	0.11
Performance evaluation	-0.11	-0.24	-0.21	-0.65	-0.74	-0.26	-0.33	-0.34	-1.21	-1.32
Performance incentives	-0.14	0.09	-0.19	0.11	-0.12	-0.32	0.32	-0.81	0.53	-0.46
Effective teaming	-0.27	-0.77	-0.91	-0.75	-1.51	-0.40	-0.93	-0.96	-1.12	-1.93
Contractor partnering	0.34	0.11	-0.12	0.48	0.47	0.46	0.22	-0.26	0.87	0.68
Air Force partnering	-0.18	0.07	-0.04	0.19	0.08	-0.26	0.09	0.07	0.06	0.05
Training in AR	0.42	0.28	0.53	0.73	1.20	0.58	0.30	0.69	0.92	1.54
Job experience	-0.04	-0.04	-0.10	-0.01	-0.09	-0.09	-0.05	-0.18	-0.05	-0.21
Product Directorate, U-2	0.02	0.63	1.47	1.32	2.47					
Adjusted R^2	0.37	0.20	0.26	0.55	0.48	0.50	0.14	0.15	0.52	0.39
F-ratio	6.76	3.54	4.45	13.4	10.12	9.15	2.37	2.39	9.66	6.21
Pr > F	<.0001	.0006	<.0001	<.0001	<.0001	<.0001	.0222	.0207	<.0001	<.0001

NOTE: Coefficients marked white with a black background have $p < 0.01$. Coefficients that are shaded medium have $p < 0.05$.
Coefficients that are shaded lightly have $p < 0.10$.

[a]Variable reported on a three-point scale. All other survey variables reported on a five-point scale.

easier to interpret in terms of variation explained by R^2 and sr^2; therefore, only they are presented here.[1]

ORDINARY LEAST SQUARES REGRESSION RESULTS

The left-hand column of Table E.1 shows the independent variable names and other statistical labels for the analyses. The columns to the right show the values of the standardized coefficients or βs, which indicate the marginal effect each organizational lever has with the number of tenets incorporated in CREP contracts, holding all other levers constant. For example, with the "simple modification" model ("simple mods"), on average, a CRT that had a highly positive attitude toward acquisition reform incorporated 0.39 more tenets in their contracts than did a CRT that had a mid-range attitude (a scale difference of one). The same CRT with a highly positive attitude toward acquisition reform incorporated 0.78 more tenets than did a CRT with a highly negative attitude (a scale difference of two or two times 0.39).[2]

Near the bottom of Table E.1 is the F-ratio, which measures the amount of variance explained by the set of independent variables. The F-ratio indicates whether the independent variables explain a significant proportion of the variance in the dependent variables. In other words, it shows whether the organizational levers could help explain contract innovation. Indeed, they explained all four sets of contract innovation groups along with the group of all CREP tenets.

---

[1]The range of our independent variables were: simple modifications, 0 to 3; key AR, 0 to 6; complete AR, 0 to 9; agile logistics, 0 to 7; all CREP tenets, 0 to 14. Figure 2.2 shows the histograms of these dependent variables. Compared to ordinary least squares analyses, the probit analyses showed improved levels of significance for several independent variables—performance evaluation, effective teaming, and contractor partnering.

[2]We note that two variables—attitude toward AR and leadership consistency—allowed only three different responses after mathematical transformation, which means CRTs can be at the most two scale intensities apart. The next five variables in Table E.1 allowed five different responses, which means CRTs can differ by as much as four scale intensities, because the variable allowed five different responses.

Also near the bottom of Table E.1 is the coefficient of determination, R^2, adjusted for the degrees of freedom.[3] R^2 measures the amount of variance in the dependent variable that the independent variables explain. Looking across the four sets of innovation groups and the group of all tenets, the agile logistics innovation group had the best fit and the organizational levers explained over half of the variance in the dependent variable (adjusted $R^2 = 0.55$). This innovation group was followed by the groups "all CREP tenets" (adjusted $R^2 = 0.48$), simple modifications (adjusted $R^2 = 0.37$), and trailed significantly by the two acquisition reform groups (adjusted $R^2 = 0.20$ and 0.26).

These results tell us that the organizational levers available to senior leadership were more related to agile logistics tenets and much less related to acquisition reform tenets. Two possible explanations are suggested. First, the organizational lever variables associated with acquisition reform may have been omitted, incomplete, or improperly measured. Second, the organizational levers the survey measured may have been intrinsically more related to agile logistics than they were to acquisition reform. We know through interviews that Warner Robins ALC emphasized two types of contract goals during the CREP initiative: (1) simple modifications for active contracts and (2) agile logistics for new contracts. Perhaps combining complicated concepts, like acquisition reform, with simpler-to-explain concepts, like agile logistics, requires a more complex approach to applying organizational levers.

T-Test Values

The t-test on the organizational lever variables in the regression analyses explains the probability that the coefficient for a particular variable is not equal to zero, i.e., it tells us whether the organizational lever had any association with the dependent variable. We considered variables as having explanatory power up to $p < 0.10$. We chose this cutoff point because our sample of 101 observations to estimate coefficients for ten independent variables is relatively small. This cutoff suggests that we risk being wrong 10 percent of the time when p-values reach 0.10.

---

[3]The R^2 value can inflate as more independent variables are added, even if they are not statistically significant. The adjusted R^2 value takes into account the addition of variables that do not have much explanatory power.

Squared Semi-Partial Correlations (sr²)

Table E.2 shows the results for the squared semi-partial correlations (sr^2) for each of the organizational lever variables. Semi-partial correlations describe the amount by which R^2 is reduced if a particular independent variable is deleted from the regression equation. In short, they explain the unique contribution of the independent variable to R^2 (Tabachnick and Fidell, 1996). The higher the value, the greater contribution the variables make toward explaining variance in the dependent variable. Except for the product directorate dummy variable, training in acquisition reform is the organizational lever variable with the single highest explanatory power. Other organizational lever variables associated with the innovation group variables are contractor partnering (for the simple modifications model), effective teaming (for the key acquisition reform concepts and agile logistics models), and performance evaluation (for the agile logistics model).

Table E.2

Results from the OLS Regression Analyses: Semi-Partial Correlations (sr^2) by Contract Innovation Group

Organizational Lever	Contract Innovation Groups (n = 101; sustainment and component repair contracts)					Contract Innovation Groups (n = 75; component repair contracts only)				
	Simple Mods	Key AR Concepts	Complete AR	Agile Logistics	All CREP Tenets	Simple Mods	Key AR Concepts	Complete AR	Agile Logistics	All CREP Tenets
Attitude toward AR[a]	0.035	0.012	0.028	0.016	0.029	0.069	0.005	0.063	0.025	0.059
Leadership consistency[a]	0.016	0.022	0.007	0.020	0.013	0.000	0.022	0.000	0.002	0.000
Performance evaluation	0.003	0.009	0.002	0.029	0.012	0.010	0.012	0.004	0.069	0.026
Performance incentives	0.003	0.000	0.000	0.000	0.000	0.007	0.005	0.012	0.006	0.001
Effective teaming	0.013	0.057	0.026	0.025	0.032	0.014	0.055	0.022	0.036	0.033
Contractor partnering	0.027	0.001	0.000	0.013	0.004	0.028	0.005	0.002	0.032	0.006
Air Force partnering	0.008	0.000	0.000	0.002	0.000	0.014	0.001	0.001	0.000	0.000
Training in AR	0.121	0.029	0.034	0.089	0.075	0.162	0.030	0.059	0.129	0.113
Job experience	0.020	0.013	0.024	0.000	0.009	0.072	0.016	0.069	0.008	0.038
Product Directorate, U-2	0.000	0.049	0.089	0.103	0.112					

[a] Variable reported on a 3-point scale. All other survey variables reported on a 5-point scale.

REFERENCES

Contract Repair Enhancement Program (CREP) Phase III Implementation: A Briefing, Warner Robins ALC, February 19, 1997.

Cronbach, L. J., "Cronbach Alpha and the Internal Structure of Tests," *Psychometrika*, Vol. 16, 1951, pp. 297–334.

DeVellis, R. F., *Scale Development: Theory and Applications, Applied Social Research Methods Series*, Vol. 26, Newbury Park, CA: Sage, 1991.

Ghoshal, S., and C. A. Bartlett, "Rebuilding Behavioral Context: A Blueprint for Corporate Renewal," *Sloan Management Review*, Winter 1996, pp. 23–36.

Hallin, Lt Gen William P., "Agile logistics: Where we've been, where we're going," *Air Force News*, April 28, 1998.

Katzenbach, J. R., and D. K. Smith, *The Wisdom of Teams*, Boston, MA: Harvard Business School Press, 1993.

Larkin, T. J., and S. Larkin, *Communicating Change: How to Win Employee Support for New Business Directions*, New York: McGraw-Hill, 1994.

Miller, Gerald, "Debt Management Networks," *Public Administration Review*, 1993, 53(1), pp. 50–58.

Moore, Nancy Y., Laura H. Baldwin, Frank Camm, and Cynthia R. Cook, *Implementing Purchasing and Supply Management*

Practices: Lessons from Innovative Commercial Firms, DB-334-AF, Santa Monica CA: RAND, 2002.

Nunnally, J. C., *Psychometric Theory*, 2nd Edition, New York: McGraw-Hill, 1978.

Pfeffer, J., "When It Comes to 'Best Practices' Why Do Smart Organizations Occasionally Do Dumb Things?" *American Management Review*, 1996, reprint.

Schaffer, R. H., and H. A. Thomson, "Successful Change Programs Begin with Results," *Harvard Business Review*, Jan–Feb 1992, pp. 80–89.

Strebel, P., "Why Do Employees Resist Change?" *Harvard Business Review*, May–June 1996, pp. 86–92.

Tabachnick, B. G., and L. S. Fidell, *Using Multivariate Statistics*, Third Edition, New York: Harper Collins, 1996.

Talking Paper on Adopting Improved Purchasing and Supply Chain Management, Headquarters U.S. Air Force, Installations and Logistics, Supply Chain Integration and Logistics Transformation (HAF/IL-I), November 25, 2002.